*Leapfrogs*

# Gymnastic Activities
## for Juniors

### Jim Hall

A & C Black · London

First published 1995 by
A & C Black (Publishers) Ltd
35 Bedford Row, London WC1R 4JH

© 1995 Jim Hall

ISBN 0 7136 4140 1

A CIP catalogue record for this book
is available from the British Library.

Cover illustration by Eleanor King

Phototypeset by Intype, London
Printed and bound in Great Britain by
Bell & Bain Limited, Thornliebank, Scotland

# CONTENTS

Let's understand Gymnastic Activities to be that indoor hall lesson which includes varied floorwork on a clear floor, unimpeded by apparatus, followed by varied apparatus work which receives just over half of the lesson time.

Ideally, the apparatus will have been positioned round the sides and ends of the room, adjacent to where it will be used. This allows each of the five or six groups of children to lift, carry and place their apparatus in a very short time because no set of apparatus will need to be moved more than 3–5 metres.

The lesson is traditionally of 30 minutes' duration, but 40 minutes would be more appropriate for Years 6 and 7.

Unlike the teaching of Geography and History, for example, where the teacher has a variety of resources to turn to, in addition to new places and centuries, the teacher of Gymnastic Activities meets the same floor and apparatus, week after week, and month after month, with the continual problem of making the lessons newly interesting, challenging, exciting and different, approximately each month.

The teacher is central to the success and enjoyment of the lessons because he or she is the source of the stimuli that make the lesson physical, educational, vigorous and enjoyable.

The following pages aim, first of all, to help provide a focus for a 'staffroom togetherness' and a unity of purpose, attitude and sense of direction among all the staff concerned with the teaching of Physical Education. Without this sense of unity, the diversity of approaches, attitudes and standards can mean that there is no continuity of expectations or programme, and a less than satisfactory level of achievement.

Secondly, the following pages provide one example of a four-year scheme of work for both junior and middle schools. There is a lesson plan and an accompanying page of explanatory notes for every month, designed to help teachers and schools with ideas for lessons which are progressive and implement NC requirements.

## Gymnastic Activities in the NC

### (1) A dual emphasis: performing and learning
• Planning: we challenge pupils to plan their actions and responses thoughtfully.
• Performing: we encourage pupils to work in a focused way, concentrating on the main feature of the task.
• Reflecting and evaluating: we assist pupils to make improvement and to progress as they adapt, change and plan again, guided by their own and others' reflections.

### (2) 'Good practice': General Requirements for all KSs
Pupils should be taught to:
(a) respond readily to instructions

(b) work hard physically and be helped to develop suppleness, strength, stamina and a healthy heart and lungs
(c) try hard to make and maintain improvement
(d) be considerate towards others
(e) maintain good posture and use the body correctly and safely
(f) lift, carry, place and use equipment safely
(g) wear appropriate clothing and be aware of the safety risks of inappropriate clothing, footwear and jewellery.

### (3) Required activities: KS2 PoS
Pupils should be taught:
(a) different ways of rolling, swinging, jump-

ing, balancing, turning and travelling on hands and feet, and how to adapt and refine these actions, both on floor and using apparatus

(b) to emphasise changes of shape, speed and direction through gymnastic actions

(c) practise, refine and repeat a longer series of actions, making increasingly complex movement sequences, both on the floor and using apparatus.

## (4) Attainment Targets End of KS Descriptions

Pupils should be able to demonstrate that they can:

(a) plan appropriate solutions, sometimes imaginatively, to the various challenges encountered

(b) work safely, alone, with a partner, and in a group

(c) practise, improve and refine performance and repeat a series of movements performed previously, with increasing control and accuracy

(d) make judgements about their own and others' performance, and use this information to improve the accuracy, quality and variety of their own performance

(e) sustain energetic activity and understand the effects of exercise on the body systems.

## Teaching Gymnastic Activities

**The teacher**, without assistance from classroom teaching aids, is the central inspiration of the lesson. An enthusiastic, well prepared teacher can inspire those wholehearted, vigorous and thoughtful responses which can lead to success, achievement and feelings of well-being and enhanced self-esteem.

**The lesson plan** is the teacher's essential guide and reminder. Only by referring to the plan can the busy teacher remind him/herself of the lesson's total content. July's end-of-year lesson will only be at a stage more advanced than the previous September's if all the lessons in between have been recorded and progressed.

**The lesson** usually runs for four to five weeks to allow children to practise, repeat, learn, remember and develop the skills involved.

**'Dead spots' and queue avoidance.** 'Be found working, not waiting' should be understood by all. Those moments when the class is standing, sitting, queuing, doing nothing, must be kept to a minimum.

**Direct teaching**, where the teacher decides what the class will do, is used to: (a) gain quick responses, good attention and class control; (b) teach the safe way to lift, carry, place and use apparatus; (c) teach the safe, correct way to perform many of the skills; (d) provide the stimulus of a direct request which most children find enjoyable, and to help the less 'inventive'; (e) concentrate on and improve poor work by making all aware of the main features in an activity.

**Shared choice or indirect teaching** is the most commonly used, and happens when the children work at activities of their choice within limits set by the teacher. With the inexperienced, the limitations imposed are very slight. 'Show me how you can travel along the bench' leaves much freedom of choice. As pupils progress, more challenging limits are placed. 'As you travel along the bench, can you include a beautifully stretched balance and a change of direction?'

Shared choice teaching results in a wide variety of responses. When accompanied by class observation and pupil and teacher comment, it rapidly increases the class repertoire.

**Demonstration, observation and comment** by the children and the teacher are an essential teaching technique. We remember what we see, and we see examples of good quality work, variety, and the safe, correct way to do things. We can also be shown the exact meaning of words and gymnastic terminology being used.

All can watch one, two or a small group. Half of the class can watch the other half. Each can watch a partner. It should be understood by the observers that they will be asked to comment after the demonstration so that it is a learning activity, which aims to assist everyone. 'Watch Susan and Gary as they do their sequences. Tell me how their work differs, and look out for changes of speed or direction that you like as interesting contrasts.'

## Apparatus work

One of four systems tends to predominate as the way individual teachers, pairs or groups of teachers, or the whole staff approach the apparatus work part of the lesson.

**System 'A'.** The apparatus is never brought out because the teacher feels insecure and incapable of organising it, and fearful for the safety of the children. The extended floorwork sessions which are substituted for the proper lessons frustrate the children who remember the excitement of apparatus work from previous years, and they behave badly making the teacher even more unwilling to risk bringing out the apparatus.

**System 'B'.** At the beginning of the morning or afternoon, before lessons start, the apparatus is brought and then left in position for every class. This system, usually put in place by 'apparatus monitors' pupils, the school caretaker, or welfare staff, whose apparatus lay-out applies to all classes:
(a) gives no credit to the intelligence and ability of children who enjoy and are perfectly capable of handling apparatus
(b) is a source of frustration to those teachers (new arrivals often) who know that it is unsatisfactory
(c) prevents the safe teaching of floorwork
(d) stifles the development of any standards

(e) breaches the NC requirement that 'Pupils should be taught how to lift, carry, place and use equipment safely.'

**System 'C'.** All classes do floorwork and apparatus work, with the apparatus being moved from a storeroom outside the hall, or from the end of the hall, assembled, used and then returned to the remote storeroom or end of hall, every lesson. This time-consuming system, with pile-ups at doors or one end of the hall, can take up to 5 minutes of the lesson time, before and after apparatus work, instead of the minute, or less, needed in the next and recommended system.

**System 'D'.** This requires the approval and co-operation of every member of staff who teaches Gymnastic Activities, and is a system that will have been initiated by the Head, the subject co-ordinator, or by a combined staff decision.

Before lessons start in the mornings or afternoons, the portable apparatus will be placed at the sides and ends of the hall, adjacent to where it will be used. By only having to lift and carry a short distance, very little time is lost by the five or six groups of five or six pupils.

From their regular starting apparatus positions, groups rotate clockwise, probably with time to work at three different sets. At the end of the apparatus work the children return to their starting places to put away the apparatus they originally brought out. Once again, little time is needed because the children are experienced in moving their own apparatus and know exactly where it has to be placed, round the sides and ends of the hall. The floor is now clear for the incoming class.

In the next lesson the groups will move anti-clockwise to work at the other three sets of apparatus.

# Safe practice and accident prevention

(1) Good supervision by the teacher at all times is the main contributor to safety in Physical Education. Being there with the class and being in positions from which to see the majority of the children is essential. In his or her circulation of the room, teaching and observing, the teacher generally will be on the outside looking inwards, to ensure that as few performers as possible are out of sight behind his or her back.

(2) Good behaviour, with its well-ordered, quiet, safe environment, must be continually insisted on until it becomes an automatic part of the lesson occasion. There is nothing for pupils to talk about, apart from on those occasions when the teacher asks for comments on a demonstration or how they think they are responding.

A clearly stated challenge or task which asks for a thoughtful, planned response precludes all chattering. Talking usually means that the class has not been given something to attend to or work towards.

The ultimate aim is a 'doubly quiet' class whose beautifully controlled and quiet movements are matched by a complete absence of inessential talking.

(3) Sensible, safe clothing means that there will be no watches, jewellery, rings, long trousers that catch heels, long sleeves that catch fingers, unbunched hair that impedes vision, or socks without shoes.

Barefoot work is recommended because it is quiet, provides a safe, strong grip on apparatus being climbed or jumped from, and it enhances the appearance of the performances, particularly when the body is inverted. The small muscles of bare feet and ankles are able to work and develop properly as they grip, stretch, balance, support, push and receive the body weight.

(4) Good teaching that develops skilled movement, confidence and self-control goes a long way to producing safe movement.

(5) A planned, written down lesson appropriate to the age of the class means that the children are always working at something specific rather than 'doing anything we like', which could include foolhardy jumping from a high bar.

(6) The development in every child of a sense of responsibility and a caring attitude towards self and others is essential and expresses itself in careful, controlled movements and a sensible sharing of floor and apparatus space.

(7) The hall should be at a good working temperature with windows and doors being closed or opened as necessary. All potentially dangerous chairs, tables, trolleys or pianos should be pushed against a wall or into a corner. Sockets for receiving securing pins of ropes and climbing frames should be regularly cleared of the cleaning substances which harden and block the sockets.

The Physical Education curriculum should enable all pupils to benefit and achieve. All children are entitled to be told how they have achieved, and to have their attainment assessed in a way that guides their future learning and progress.

The AT – End of KS Descriptions briefly identify the types and range of performance that the majority of pupils should characteristically demonstrate by the end of the KS.

Three headings serve to summarise the areas within which we want our pupils to achieve within the framework of the NC.

• **Performing** successfully is the main aim. In a satisfactory performance a pupil demonstrates:
(a) well-controlled, neat and accurate work
(b) the ability to practise to improve skilfulness
(c) the ability to perform skills safely
(d) the ability to link actions together with control
(e) wholehearted and vigorous activity, sharing the space sensibly and unselfishly, with a concern for own and others' safety
(f) a capacity for skilfulness, variety and versatility
(g) pleasure from participating enthusiastically and confidently.

• **Planning** thoughtfully precedes the performance as the pupil thinks ahead to what his or her response will be, trying to 'see' the intended outcome. Evidence of satisfactory planning can be seen in:
(a) good decision-making and thinking ahead with appropriate actions

(b) sensible, safe judgements
(c) good understanding of what was asked for
(d) a willingness to listen to and adapt to others' views
(e) an understanding of the elements that enhance quality, variety and contrast in 'movement'
(f) the expression of positive personal qualities such as optimism, enthusiasm, and a capacity for hard work in pursuit of improvement.

• **Evaluating and reflecting** by the observant teacher, by oneself, and by pupils after observing a demonstration, help to inspire and guide pupils as they adapt, alter, develop and improve their work. Friendly, helpful, positive comments encourage and uplift the performer, and the observers benefit from the comments and guidance given. Where standards in evaluating are satisfactory, pupils can:
(a) see and identify the different actions taking place
(b) describe the most important features
(c) express pleasure at the part of the performance they liked
(d) comment on the accuracy and success of the work
(e) reflect sensitively with a concern for another's feelings
(f) suggest ways to bring about an improvement
(g) self-evaluate and act upon their own reflections.

# Fixed and portable apparatus

In the lesson plans that follow, the equipment continually being referred to and shown in apparatus lay-outs includes the following items:

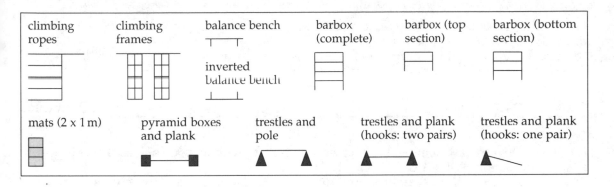

## Minimum number recommended
- 12 × mats (2 × 1 m).
- 3 × balance benches.
- 1 × barbox which can be divided into two smaller boxes by lifting off the top section. The remaining lower section should have a platform fitted.
- 1 × pair pyramid boxes and one plank.
- 1 × pair of 3 ft (0.9 m), 3 ft 6 in (1 m), and 4 ft 6 in (1.4 m) trestles.
- 1 metal pole to join pairs of trestles.
- 2 planks with two pairs hooks.
- 2 planks with one pair hooks.

## LESSON PLAN • 30 MINUTES

At the start of the year the lesson's main emphases include:

(a) creating a safe, quiet, co-operative environment where all work together sensibly and unselfishly, particularly in sharing space
(b) establishing a tradition of immediate responses to instructions
(c) co-operating with others to lift, carry, assemble, share and then put away the apparatus.

## FLOORWORK                                                          12 minutes

### Legs
(1) Show me your best running, keeping well away from others. When I call 'Stop!' stand in a space by yourself, not near anyone or any of the apparatus at the sides and ends. Stop!
(2) Visit every part of the room, the sides, ends and the middle. Remember that good running is quiet and you don't follow anyone. Stop!
### Body
(1) Just where you are, show me a big high jump with a strong swing up in your arms and a nice, 'squashy' landing, softly on both feet, by letting your ankles, knees and hips 'give'.
(2) Can you contrast the firm, strong stretch up with the more gentle, light and 'easy' actions in your landings?
### Arms
(1) Look for a space, then move, travelling slowly on hands and feet. Can you show me your travelling actions clearly?
(2) Hands can travel by themselves, then feet by themselves, or they can all work together.

## APPARATUS WORK                                                     16 minutes

(1) Travel to all parts of the room without touching any apparatus other than mats. When I call 'Stop!' show me a fully stretched body shape on the nearest piece of apparatus. Stop!
(2) When I call 'Stop!' next time, can you show me your stretch on a different body part on a different piece of apparatus? Stop!
(3) Now use your feet only to show me how you can get on to, along and then away from the apparatus.
(4) Use hands and feet both on the apparatus and the floor in between to show me some of your favourite ways to travel.
(5) Return to your number one apparatus places, ready to put away the same apparatus that you brought out.
(6) Quietly, carefully and sensibly, please put your apparatus back to its position round the sides and ends of the room.

## FINAL FLOOR ACTIVITY                                                2 minutes

Once again, show me your best running where you follow no-one and where you visit all parts of the room.

## NC requirements being emphasised

(a) Being taught to be physically active.
(b) Working safely, alone and with others.

## FLOORWORK

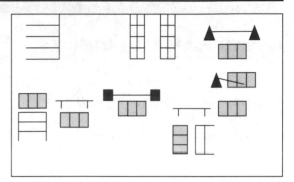

**Legs** (1) For 'best running', ask for lifting of heels, knees, arms and head for lightness and quietness. The 'Stop!' gives practice in making immediate response. (2) Ask for straight line running to counter the curving, anti-clockwise running, common among primary school pupils, with all following and impeding all.

**Body** (1) In the air, stretch everything from arms above head right down to toes and ankles pointing. This contrasts with the 'give' in those joints for a soft, quiet landing. (2) Ankles are often under exercised with little mobility resulting. 'Really push with your feet and drive hard to stretch your ankles fully at take-off and in the air.'

**Arms** (1) Travelling should be done slowly to show the actions clearly and exercise the parts strongly. No quick scampering! (2) In addition to the usual head first with tummy towards the floor travelling, we can lead with feet or one side, and we can travel with back, front or side towards the floor.

## APPARATUS WORK

(Preceded by teacher's 'Please go to your number one apparatus places.' Then 'Quietly and sensibly, please bring out your apparatus.') (1) Circulation is to 'all parts of the room, along straight lines, never following anyone and listening for my signal to stop.' (2) Stopping and showing a fully stretched body on the nearest apparatus is an exercise in listening and responding immediately. (3) 'Feet only' means easy steps, jumps, swings on to apparatus; then steps, runs, jumps or bounces along and from. Ropes are not used because they need hands. Use of climbing frames is limited. (4) Hands and feet travel on floor and apparatus includes going on, under, around, across; gripping, pulling, circling, climbing, rolling and vaulting on narrow, wide, low, high surfaces. (5) 'Number one apparatus' is that which a group brings out. They know where it starts from, at the side or end of the room, and they are experienced in lifting and carrying it. (6) The lift and carry of apparatus by a well trained, well behaved class takes less than a minute, and the floor is left clear for the next class to do its floorwork, safely and unimpeded.

## FINAL FLOOR ACTIVITY

The class should be asked to 'Feel the lifting in your knees and heels for quietness. Pretend you have chalk on your feet and leave your straight line footprints all over the space.'

**11**

## LESSON PLAN • 30 MINUTES

### LESSON THEME AND MAIN EMPHASES

(a) Neat, controlled, natural activities.   (b) Body parts awareness; understanding of how body propels/receives/supports body weight.

### FLOORWORK                                                    12 minutes

**Legs** (1) Practise quiet, soft upward jumps on the spot. Show me a good stretch in your ankles when you push up, and let ankles and knees 'give' on landing.   (2) Now walk or run carefully a few steps until you see a good space, then show me another upward jump and soft landing.   (3) Show me other favourite ways to travel, using feet only.

**Body** (1) Different parts of your body can support you as you move. Start off on your seat and show me how you can change from part to part (e.g. from seat roll to back; twist or roll on to tummy; curl to kneeling; to side falling on one hand, one foot).   (2) Can you 'feel' the different actions you are using to move?

**Arms** (1) As you travel slowly using hands and feet, can you include moments when all the weight is on your hands?   (2) Try to use hands and feet equally; hands, then feet alternately; and try hands and feet wide, then close together.

### APPARATUS WORK                                               16 minutes

(1) Use neat feet actions only as you travel to all parts of room, without touching any apparatus. Can you travel without stopping by using different actions to suit where you are?

(2) You can walk when you have to go slowly under, through, across; run when there is clear floor; and jump over low apparatus such as mats, benches and planks. Can you show me any other favourite ways to travel, using feet only, and not touching apparatus?

(3) Using feet or feet and hands, change now to travelling up to, on, along, then from the apparatus. Travel slowly to show me your actions clearly. As well as moving from apparatus to apparatus, can you think of the varied actions it is possible to include? (For instance, climbing; circling; hanging; rolling; sliding; balancing; springing; pulling.)

(4) For a change, can you try some travelling on body parts other than, or in addition to hands and feet? A balance with a move to a new balance is a good way to practise (e.g. on seat; rock back to shoulders; twist legs back over one shoulder on to kneeling; roll sideways, back to sitting).

### FINAL FLOOR ACTIVITY                                         2 minutes

Walk, run, jump with a nicely stretched body, then land silently by letting your legs 'give'. Be still for a moment, then start again.

## NC requirements being emphasised

(a) Exploring different means of taking weight on hands, and jumping.
(b) Responding readily to instructions.

## FLOORWORK

**Legs** (1) Feel the body tension from top of head right down to strongly stretched ankles in the jump, and then the contrasting, relaxed, 'giving' in knees, ankles and hips on landing. (2) 'A few steps' only, because the jumping and landing are the important parts. They can try one- and two-footed take-offs. (3) Teacher commentary will identify the class repertoire to spread the range of activities being used.

**Body** (1) Body parts travelling is more unusual and difficult than travelling on feet or hands and feet. Much experimentation and good use of demonstrations are needed. (2) Linking movements to be 'felt' include rolling, leaning, sitting, lowering, twisting, rocking, springing, tilting.

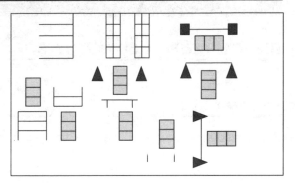

**Arms** (1) Once again, teacher commentary will identify the many ways to travel, slowly, on hands and feet. 'Crawling; one side then the other; hands only, then feet only; bunny jump; cartwheel; wide hands and feet; close hands and feet; handwalking.' (2) They can bounce up and down on all fours, equally. Hands and feet alternately in cartwheels. Hands and feet wide for a difficult, strong action. Hands and feet close for a high, arching travel.

## APPARATUS WORK

(1) Non-stop action with lots of running in open spaces; jumping over mats, across mats, benches and low planks; walking in congested, difficult areas; and own favourite extras. (2) The emphasis is on negotiating apparatus without touching any yet, and looking ahead to find quiet places. (3) Feet, or feet and hands to bring you on; hands or hands and feet to travel on, around, across, below, climb up, roll on or around; then a neat spring off. Ask them to think of all the words that describe their many and varied actions. Good demonstrations by a versatile trio or quartet can be used to elicit lots of action words. 'Observers, put your hand up as a signal that you can name four different actions in these excellent demonstrations.' (4) Travelling on many body parts, practised earlier in the floorwork, should inspire rocking and rolling on the back, spinning on the seat, twisting and rolling on the whole stretched, lying body and twisting over on the shoulders.

## FINAL FLOOR ACTIVITY

A series of three, linked actions with the emphasis on body shape, and good still, starting and finishing positions. 'Land and be still. Look for a new space where you will not disturb anyone, and off you go again.'

## LESSON PLAN • 30 MINUTES

### LESSON THEME

Body shape awareness in held positions and on the move. Awareness of long, wide, curled or twisted shapes within own performances and those of others. Shape's contribution to good style, efficiency of movements, and strong work.

### FLOORWORK                                            12 minutes

**Legs** (1) After a neat, still, tall start, walk, run and jump up into a beautifully stretched position. Land softly and show stillness again in a tall, stretched body position. (2) You can take off from one or both feet, and you can land on alternate or both feet. Landing one foot after the other helps you to slow down and control the whole landing. (3) Where are your arms on landing to help your balance? Try a sideways and a forward stretch of both arms.
**Body** (1) Using different body supporting parts, can you change from wide stretches to tight curls? (e.g. from standing, feet and arms stretched wide; to crouched position, with feet close together; to back lying with arms and legs wide; to curled small on shoulders, hands clasped under knees; to a long roll forward on to wide hands and feet, etc.) (2) Can you plan and practise a little sequence of slow, almost non-stop movements?
**Arms** (1) Practise 'bunny jumps' with arms straight, legs kept bent. (2) For a contrast, can you lift your feet in the air, legs stretched, on one, two or alternate hands?

### APPARATUS WORK                                       16 minutes

(1) Run in and out of all the apparatus, but don't touch any until I say 'Stop!' Then show me a clear body shape on the nearest piece of apparatus. Stop!
(2) Next time, when I signal, try to show me a body shape that contrasts with the others who are sharing your apparatus. Stop!
(3) Can you travel up to a piece of apparatus and arrive on it with your body curled. Travel on the different surfaces and include contrasting body shapes as you go. Leave your apparatus and show me a beautifully stretched, still body before moving off to your next piece of apparatus.
(4) Stay at your present piece of apparatus with no more than four others. Start and finish in a still, stretched position on the floor away from apparatus. Within your travelling on floor and apparatus, can you plan to include: (a) a run and jump; (b) a variety of shapes as you travel; (c) weight on hands somewhere?

### FINAL FLOOR ACTIVITY                                  2 minutes

Can you travel all round with a leg or legs sometimes stretched?

## NC requirements being emphasised

(a) Demonstrating changes of shape through gymnastic actions.

(b) Making judgements of performance and suggesting ways to improve.

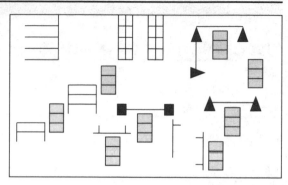

## FLOORWORK

**Legs** (1) The 'beautifully stretched' position in flight extends from long, upstretched arms above head, all the way down to the fully and strongly extended ankles. This clear shape looks good and is hard work compared with a limp, lazy, sagging performance. (2) The emphasis moves to how the feet are operating. A two-footed take-off helps an upward jump (one foot helps a long jump) and the alternate foot landing is the best for a gradual, slow landing. (3) Like the long pole of a tight rope walker, the stretched arms help us to maintain our balance in landing.

**Body** (1) The linking movements between the stretches and the curls are important. Pupils need to be aware of rolling, rocking, lowering, springing up, twisting, sitting, lying, arching, upending, levering. (2) Three movements are sufficient for interest and as a challenge. Also of interest are different levels as we stand, sit, lie, arch, become upended.

**Arms** (1) In bunny jumps, keep the arms straight for strength and safety, legs bent for a quick lift up, and head looking forward so that everything appears the right way up. Perfection is a straight line through shoulders, hips and hands, with fingers pointing forward. (2) We start the bunny jump from a crouched position on hands and feet. The 'legs stretched' activities will start from standing with a swing up forward to handstand or sideways into cartwheels.

## APPARATUS WORK

(1) Whole body should be involved in the 'clear body shape', where we encourage a variety of supporting parts, not always the feet. (2) Those with whom you are contrasting do not always know of this contrasting relationship. They might be relating to another. (3) In travelling through contrasting shapes on the apparatus, try to recall some of the linked actions on the floor, earlier. (4) In the last apparatus sequence requested, the 'weight on hands' can come at start on floor. 'Run and jump' can be at the end, coming away from apparatus. Curling to stretching is an easy way to travel on, around, along, under or across apparatus.

## FINAL FLOOR ACTIVITY

One or both legs stretched while stepping, leaping up or forward, jumping to turn in the air, slipping sideways with an upward lift, bouncing travelling with a full stretch in flight.

## LESSON PLAN • 30 MINUTES

### LESSON THEME

(a) Space awareness and knowing where you and others are going as you share the floor and apparatus space, together.
(b) Using own and general space, with different directions, levels and pathways to improve the variety and quality of the work.

### FLOORWORK                                                    12 minutes

**Legs** (1) In your own, small space, can you run with high knee raising? Then show me normal running, using the whole floor space. (2) Can you add a little pathway, such as a circle, oval or figure 8, in your space, then repeat that pathway in the whole room space?
**Body** (1) Can you travel at different levels, and even in different directions, by bringing parts of your body together, then taking them apart? (e.g. back lying, legs and arms wide; close legs and arms, roll long body sideways on to back again; curl in small, hands clasped under knees; rock back on to stretched shoulder balance, legs apart; long rock forward to standing, etc.) (2) Plan a short sequence to include each of the three levels.
**Arms** (1) This half of the class will travel on feet and hands along straight line pathways, with a stretched body for most of the time. The other half will travel, on feet and hands also, along curving or rounded pathways and you will try to bring parts of your body together and take them apart as you travel. (2) Remember that you can have your back, front or one side towards the floor, and you can lead with parts other than head.

### APPARATUS WORK                                               16 minutes

(1) Travel freely on floor and all apparatus, and include a direction change, either at start, finish, or within your travelling on the apparatus.
(2) Show me how you can approach each piece of apparatus, going forwards, and leave it, facing sideways or, very carefully, backwards.

(3) Can you try to include different levels at which you can travel or hold a still position, on apparatus and floor? (For example, high, standing on a box; medium, arched on a plank; low, body close to a bench or box.)

### FINAL FLOOR ACTIVITY                                         2 minutes

Make a pattern of jumping where you include movement on the spot and either forward, sideways, backwards or diagonally.

## NC requirements being emphasised

(a) Practising, developing, refining and repeating a longer series of actions, making increasingly complex movement sequences on the floor and apparatus.

(b) Demonstrating changes of direction and level through gymnastic actions.

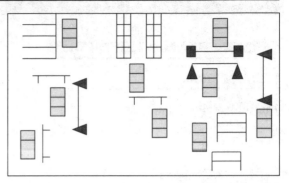

## FLOORWORK

**Legs** (1) An exercise in using own, personal space and the general, whole room space. In own space, upright body, with knees up to waist high and ankles pointed down, for about 8 counts, alternate with a circuit of the room back to own space. (2) Demonstrate with good performers, asking the observers to 'Look out for and tell me which pathways were very clear.'

**Body** (1) Try to include the more difficult high and medium levels, in addition to the easier low level. (High cartwheel from standing, feet and hands together into the star shape travel, feet and hands wide; leaping from feet together into one foot after the other. Medium travel on straight arms and legs, travelling arms only, then feet only, arching then flattening.) (2) For example – high cart-wheel, opening and closing arms and legs; medium hands and feet, alternately arching and spreading hands and feet; low curl on back alternate with stretch and roll sideways.

**Arms** (1) A 'mostly stretched body' can be cartwheels, handwalking, long straight arms and legs crouched travelling, bouncing along on all fours with body long and straight. 'Body parts coming together and parting' can be crouched, hands only travel then jump feet to catch up, or walk arms forward only, then walk feet forward only. (2) Unless the teacher suggests it, or demonstrates otherwise, most will always travel with body towards floor and head leading.

## APPARATUS WORK

(1) Direction changes can include: steps and jumps forwards and sideways; rolls forward, sideways and backwards; hanging and travel-ling sideways and backwards; hands on to vault on facing forward and come off facing backwards or sideways; on hands and feet easily facing in all directions. (2) A momentary stay on apparatus, concerned principally with the immediate arrival and the departure. 'On, going forwards' includes steps, jumps, swings, rolls, levering off as in bunny jump with a twist to side. (3) High level, often on feet or hanging from arms, stretched, plus high jumps; medium, crab arched, or horizontal balance on one foot or across a bar; low, near to surface travelled on.

## FINAL FLOOR ACTIVITY

A triangular pattern can include four skip jumps on the spot, then four diagonally forward, then four diagonally backward, then four to side and back to starting place.

# Year 3 • January • Lesson 5

## LESSON PLAN • 30 MINUTES

### LESSON THEME

Jumping, rolling, balancing.

### FLOORWORK                                                    12 minutes

**Legs** (1) Do small jumps where you are. Keep your body straight, but let your knees bend to make the landing soft and quiet. (2) Using a very short run, go round the room, jumping up from one or both feet. Body straight in the air, and a nice 'squashy' landing, with a good bend in your knees. (3) Use stretched arms to help your balanced landing. Arms can stretch forward, sideways or straight upwards.

**Body** (1) Lie on your back, curled up small, and roll back and forwards from seat all the way to your shoulders and hands. (2) Now, with hands clasped under knees, still curled up on your back, can you roll from side to side? (3) Can you start, crouched; lower into a roll back and forward: roll from side to side; then rock back and strongly forward and up on to feet?

**Arms** (1) With a long swing of arms from above head, can you try to balance on your hands? (2) Try an elbow balance. From a crouch position with feet apart, place hands on floor, shoulder width apart and under shoulders. Bend elbows slightly to place them inside and under knees. Tilt body weight forward from feet.

**Floor sequence** Plan and practise a jump on the spot; run and high jump with a well balanced landing; lower down on to seat; roll back and strongly forward back to standing; swing up on to hands or finish with an elbow balance.

### APPARATUS WORK                                              16 minutes

(1) As you travel all round the room without touching apparatus, can you include jumps across mats, over benches and low planks?

(2) When I call 'Stop!' show me a balance on the nearest piece of apparatus, or apparatus and floor. Stop!

(3) Travel freely on floor and apparatus. You may roll on mats, and from apparatus. With a nicely stretched body, can you jump off the apparatus, land softly, and lower into a smooth sideways roll?

(4) Now stay at your present piece of apparatus to practise, repeat and improve the following: (a) Start and finish on the floor, away from the apparatus; (b) travel up to, on, along and away from your apparatus and show me . . .; (c) jumps, rolls and, somewhere, a beautifully still balance with a clear body shape.

### FINAL FLOOR ACTIVITY                                         2 minutes

Balance on tip toes with arms stretched. Run, jump and land with a well-balanced finish, with straight arms again helping your balance.

## NC requirements being emphasised

(a) Exploring different means of rolling, jumping and balancing.
(b) Making appropriate decisions quickly and planning responses.

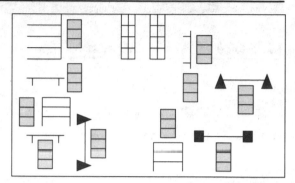

## FLOORWORK

**Legs** (1) The jumps on the spot should be quiet with ankles and knees 'giving' like springs to absorb the shock. Ankles are often weak and underused and full stretches of ankles need to be pursued, with lots of practice. (2) The body tension in the air, with firmness felt throughout, is in contrast to the more giving, gentle feeling on landing. (3) If jump tends to be high, arms stretched sideways helps the balance. If jump is long, arms forward helps the balance.

**Body** (1) The short rock back on to hands is like the start of a backward roll. The push forward with hands is like the end of a forward roll. In both, keep well rounded with head on chest. (2) In side to side rolls, with hands tightly clasped under knees, feel the swing of legs and hands to start the rolling actions. (3) The lower, roll back and forward is an easy movement. The roll sideways is an easy movement. The rock back to a strong push with hands and the rock up on to feet is the hardest movement.

**Arms** (1) Arms are straight for a safe, strong support. The head faces forward because looking back under arms makes everything appear to be upside down. Feet together in the handstand is difficult to hold. It is easier to balance with one leg ahead, one back, making a long, low, straight line, like a tight rope walker's pole. (2) The difficulty here is to hold the slight bend in the elbows. Keep the bend as slight as possible or arms give too easily.

## APPARATUS WORK

(1) There will be simple, low jumps over part of a mat; higher jumps over benches and low planks; and there can be bounding, two-footed jumps along the length of a bench or plank. (2) 'Balance' means that your body is on some small or unusual body support and not wobbling, which it wants to do. (3) The full forward rolls which will happen should have the head tucked well under so that arms, then shoulders and back receive the body (not the head), by a gradual bending of the arms. (4) The final apparatus sequence of jumping, rolling and balancing has an attractive variety of explosive, energetic jumps, smooth, flowing rolls, and still, firm balance. With a group sharing the apparatus, working almost non-stop, this can be very exciting to take part in, and to observe as a group demonstration.

## FINAL FLOOR SEQUENCE

From balanced, still start to balanced, still finish will be only a few metres, being careful not to intrude on others' space. Deter long, long runs before the jumps.

## LESSON PLAN • 30 MINUTES

### LESSON THEME

Sequences, and planning to link together a short series of actions on floor and apparatus with poised beginnings, middles and ends.

### FLOORWORK                                                     12 minutes

**Legs**
(1) Using your legs, plan to show me a triangle of movements, starting and finishing at the same place on the floor.
(2) Can you include three different actions in your travelling, take-offs or landings?
(3) Emphasise clear, firm body shapes throughout. No sagging!

**Body**
(1) In your own floor space, can you plan a short sequence of some of your favourite balances?
(2) Can you plan to include varied supporting parts?
(3) Working at different levels looks particularly good.

**Arms**
(1) Slowly and quietly, travel on hands and feet.
(2) Think about the actions you are doing and try to include at least three that are contrasting (e.g. cartwheel; on all fours with stretched arms and legs; hands first, then legs with a twist).

### APPARATUS WORK                                               16 minutes

(1) As you visit each different set of apparatus in turn, can you repeat a pattern of travelling up to, on and off quickly to a finishing place on the floor? Your finishing place becomes your starting place for your next practice, using a different set of apparatus.
(2) Now expand your sequence by including a balance and weight on hands, which can take place on apparatus, floor, or a combination of the two.
(3) Now stay at your present group with no more than five others sharing, to plan, repeat, practise and improve the following sequence:

(a) start and finish on the floor away from apparatus
(b) include at least two ways of travelling on feet
(c) include a firm, clear body shape within a balance, and
(d) include hands and feet travelling, which can be on floor; along, across, around, under apparatus; or using both floor and apparatus.

### FINAL FLOOR SEQUENCE                                          2 minutes

Practise again your triangle of leg activities and show me three different, clear, firm body shapes. Demonstrating the shapes while in flight is most spectacular, but you can also include them as part of your starting and finishing positions.

## NC requirements being emphasised

(a) Practising, adapting, improving and repeating longer and increasingly complex sequences of movement.

(b) Working vigorously to develop suppleness, strength, stamina and to exercise the heart and lungs strongly.

## FLOORWORK

**Legs** (1) Establish your own triangle space, with 3-metre sides and small enough not to impede others. (2) Aim for variety and attractive contrast within the trio. This variety is evident in the nature of the actions and any take-offs and landings (e.g. from and to one, both or alternate feet). (3) Clear body shapes enhance the appearance and efficiency of the movements, and make our bodies work hard to achieve them.

**Body** (1) Done in own floor space, slowly and thoughtfully, focusing on how to link them together, with, ideally, the non-supporting parts stretching strongly. (2) You can be standing, sitting, kneeling, upended on shoulders, in a crab arch, or side on to floor on one hand and one foot. (3) High level can be on one foot or tip toes; medium on one foot with body horizontal, on a difficult crab; low, near floor on elbow and hand, or sitting, feet and arms off floor.

**Arms** (1) A 'sequence' needs at least two different actions, neatly linked and able to be repeated. (2) 'Contrasting' from varied actions of parts concerned; levels shown; body shape, changing or not; from parts towards floor, front, back or side; from parts leading, head, feet or one side.

## APPARATUS WORK

(1) Whole class, well spaced, can travel clockwise from a starting set of apparatus to the next one, practising a still beginning and end and a very short, snappy middle on to and from apparatus. (2) Check they understand meanings of 'expand' and making their sequences bigger now, by adding a balance and taking weight on hands. Still ask for clockwise movement, and still, well controlled starts and finishes, signifying 'I am about to start' and 'I am finished.' (3) We stay at the one set of apparatus to allow much repetition and improvement to take place. Much travelling on feet, probably at start and finish. What actions? Some hands and feet travelling, particularly on difficult surfaces. Above, below, across, around? At least one firm, clear body shape within a balance. How difficult can you make it and still be in control of your self?

## FINAL FLOOR ACTIVITY

The range of possible body shapes includes being long and stretched; wide, like a star, and stretched; curled and round; arched to front, side or rear; twisted, with one body part working against another.

## LESSON PLAN • 30 MINUTES

### LESSON THEME

Body shape awareness in stillness and in movement, and understanding body shape's contribution to quality and making the work more demanding. Limp or sagging is lazy and unattractive.

### FLOORWORK                                                    12 minutes

**Legs** (1) Can you travel with one or both legs sometimes stretched? (2) Stretching can take place in the air and during actions such as stretched leg walking, running, bouncing or slipping sideways.

**Body** (1) Can you show me three bridge-like shapes, neatly linked? (2) You can be high on feet or tip toes; medium in a side towards floor position on one hand and one foot; and low in a sitting or arching position. Try to use different levels. (3) Try to be aware of the linking actions you are using – rolling, twisting, lowering, springing, levering, rocking, etc.

**Arms** (1) With hands on floor, can you jump your feet up into the air, kicking them past each other strongly? This can be called 'kicking horses.' (2) Try to keep your legs stretched as you kick them past each other. This action seems to help us to keep our balance.

### APPARATUS WORK                                               16 minutes

**Ropes** What body shapes can you show me using two ropes?

**Climbing frames** Can you twist as you travel? Contrast this with a still scissors shape somewhere.

**Mats** Practise again to improve your floorwork sequence of three bridge-like shapes, using mats to try more adventurous linking movements and bridges.

**Trestles, pole, planks** Make bridge-like shapes on different parts of the apparatus, or apparatus and floor.

**Box top, pyramid boxes and plank, mats** Try to work together as a group, moving from piece to piece of apparatus, holding a firm, clear shape which changes with your changing of places.

**Box base, benches, mats** These low surfaces will allow much jumping and landing to take place. Show your clear shape in flight and try to contrast this held, firm shape with a moving body shape (e.g. a long, slow roll; a crouched 'bunny jump' across).

### FINAL FLOOR ACTIVITY                                          2 minutes

Walk, run and jump, using your arms well and strongly to show me a clear body shape in the air – stretched, wide, long, curled, tucked or twisted.

## NC requirements being emphasised

(a) Emphasising changes of shape through gymnastic actions.

(b) Making judgements of performances and suggesting ways to improve.

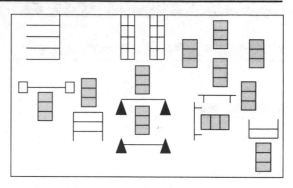

## FLOORWORK

**Legs** (1) Emphasise the 'travelling' and the 'sometimes stretched', as they experiment with both. (2) Stretching high within flight will include any long, wide sideways or front to rear extension of the legs (hurdling action). At a lower level we can stretch leg or legs as we walk, run, gallop, bounce, hop, hopscotch, skip or slip, opening and closing feet sideways.

**Body** (1) Ask class to identify examples of bridge-like shapes in the room to guide them, e.g. trestles, arch of ceiling, bench. (2) Bridge can be under, behind or to one side of the body, nearly always supported on two body parts, at least. (3) The linking movements should be done slowly as you transfer your weight from body parts to body parts, often involving an element of balancing.

**Arms** (1) In earlier lessons they will have practised bent leg bunny jumps, straight leg handstands, and split legs handstands, without the legs moving in the balance position. (2) As well as being another activity to practise while weight is on hands, the kicking back and forward of both legs seems to help with the balancing.

## APPARATUS WORK

**Ropes** Climb two, stretching and curling, swing with body wide curled or tucked; circle round from standing back to standing. **Climbing frames** Twist by having a fixed point and working against it. Fix hands on bar, twist legs through space. Fix feet, twist upper body to pull to sitting. **Mats** Handstands, walk over into crab arch; and headstand, tilt over into crab, are two more adventurous examples possible on mats. **Trestles** Bridges on feet on floor, hands against part of apparatus; on top of mat or plank surfaces; arched on pole. **Box, pyramid boxes and plank** Balancing group on many body parts on many apparatus parts. Leader of group sets rhythm for group.

(a) Arrive on, move slowly into balance with strong, firm shape. (b) Slowly, move out of balance to next piece to repeat, ideally, on new body part with new clear shape. **Box, bench** Flight with a held shape. Then travel in contact with floor and/or apparatus in a shape that lets you travel, such as a roll.

## FINAL FLOOR ACTIVITY

A triangle with short, 3-metre sides, to demonstrate shapes in flight, is attractive and interesting.

## LESSON PLAN • 30 MINUTES

### LESSON THEME

Partner work to: (a) provide new experiences not possible on one's own; (b) extend powers of observation, both of own and partner's choice of activities; (c) inspire enjoyable, desirable, co-operative social relationships.

### FLOORWORK                                                        12 minutes

**Legs** (1) One partner will show the other a simple floor pattern of leg activities in own floor space. (2) Can you make your pattern of walking, running, jumping, skipping and any other activities short enough for your partner to copy and do along with you, in unison? (3) Now the other partner will lead in leg activities that use the whole floor space and return you both to your starting places. (4) Finally, combine the two sets of travelling without stopping in between.

**Body** (1) From a starting one leading, one following, can you build up to matching work in: from standing, sit curled small, rock back on to shoulders and hands, rock forward through sitting back up to standing? (2) Variety can come from starting arms position in standing, from feet and leg positions throughout, and from your clear and changing body shapes.

**Arms** (1) Partner A makes various bridges supported on hands and feet. Partner B travels under and around the bridges, using hands and feet only. (2) Change over duties. Remember that you can have front, back or side towards the floor.

### APPARATUS WORK                                                   16 minutes

(1) One leading, one following from a noted starting place on the floor. Travel up to each group of apparatus in turn and travel on it. Finish in your starting position. Now see if the following partner can remember where you went and all the ways of travelling that were used on floor and apparatus. (2) Show your partner a way of using hands to bring you on to a piece of apparatus. Now show your partner a way of leaving the apparatus where your feet are important. Travel around to the different pieces of apparatus. (3) Now stay at one piece of apparatus with your partner and no more than two couples. Can your pair plan, practise and work up to: (a) travelling from opposite sides up to, on, along, and from the apparatus in unison; (b) including a balance, roll and a jump somewhere, and; (c) finishing in your partner's starting position?

### FINAL FLOOR ACTIVITY                                             2 minutes

Face partner. One leads in a simple jumping routine of feet opening and closing sideways and/or forwards to 4 or 8 counts.

## NC requirements being emphasised
(a) Working safely, alone and with others.
(b) Trying hard to consolidate performances.

## FLOORWORK

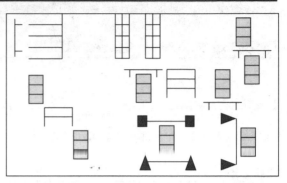

**Legs** (1) Follower notes the actions and what the body parts are doing, first of all, e.g. stepping on tip toes. Next, look for body shape, then any direction changes being used, e.g. tip toe walking with high knees and straight arms, forwards, backwards and sideways. (2) Three actions are enough to observe and copy, at one time. (3) Leading partner will lead along straight lines, not curving, following along behind others. (4) Partners face each other on the spot, then follow around the whole room space, keeping about 2 metres apart for both.

**Body** (1) The changing levels, high standing, low sitting, medium on shoulders add an interesting contrast, as will slow, well-controlled, varied linking movements. (2) Long stretched standing to curled sitting to wide stretched on shoulders, with body working hard to show clear, firm shapes.

**Arms** (1) Holding, bridge making partner must give weaving partner plenty of room. Held positions vary from easy high on tip toes with body arched to hard low, side on to floor, on one hand and one foot. (2) Feet and hand combinations include wide apart, close together, two and one, one and two, one and one, back, front or side to floor.

## APPARATUS WORK

(1) While leader has to plan where to go and what to include, the follower has to plan to observe... What actions and uses of body parts? What body shapes? What directions? At a more advanced level with a good class, they would also be considering... What effort? What speeds? What amounts of force? (2) 'Hands on, feet off' means following at about 2–3 metres to give leader room, and to be able to observe efficiently. Leader going and waiting while follower catches up, might be helpful. (3) Partners now remain at the same apparatus setting to be able to 'repeat, adapt, improve and repeat a longer series of actions'. Three group places should be possible in one lesson for variety.

## FINAL FLOOR ACTIVITY

Leading partner can quietly say the actions 'Side, in, side, in; left forward, right forward, left forward, right forward; side, in, side, in' as they perform their two part pattern.

## LESSON PLAN • 30 MINUTES

### LESSON THEME

(a) Jumping, rolling and balancing. (b) Using right amount of effort for each task.

### FLOORWORK                                                            12 minutes

**Legs** (1) Balanced on tip toes, stretch tall with arms and heels high. Use a short run into a space near you, jump up high, land with a soft squashy action, then lower to lying, curled up small. Roll sideways right over on to hands and feet. Return to balance standing on tip toes and repeat. (2) Can you contrast your strong upward jump with a soft, quiet, slow lowering to back lying?
**Body** (1) Show me a 'firm' balance, where your whole body is working hard to show a clear shape with no wobbling. Now contrast this firmness with a relaxed, gentle moving on to another part or parts to balance strongly again. (2) How are you linking the balances? You can roll, curl, twist, lower, lever, spin, spring.
**Arms** (1) Try a long, slow swing of the arms from above your head up into a handstand. Balance is helped by letting one leg stay back and one reach forward to make almost a straight line with your legs. (Like a tight rope walker's pole.) (2) Keep your arms straight and head facing well forward.

### APPARATUS WORK                                                        16 minutes

**Ropes** Can you join together a balanced starting position, a strong swing, and flowing roll to finish? **Climbing frames** Show me a balance on one frame, roll to other frame, and show me a second balance. **Benches** Show me contrasting ways to use the benches as springboards. For example, accelerate up to a vigorous drive from one, and a gentle push off and flowing action from the other. You may finish with a roll on the mats. **Trestle** each. Show me parts of the trestle on which you can hold a balance. After 2 or 3 seconds, change to a different part of you or your tres-tle to hold a new balance. Every time, make your shape firm and clear with your body working hard to keep this tension. **Pyramid boxes and bench** Start and finish, beautifully balanced, standing on the floor. Travel up to, on to, along or across your apparatus, and leave with a strong upward jump and landing, lowering into a sideways roll. **Boxes** As a group, demonstrate a variety of balances using mats, boxes, or boxes and mats. As a group also, can you vary levels, body shapes and supporting parts?

### FINAL FLOOR ACTIVITY                                                   2 minutes

Stand still, no fidgeting, but relaxed and with no body tension. Accelerate into an explosive leap and land in a strongly balanced position. Relax and repeat.

## NC requirements being emphasised

(a) Exploring different means of rolling, balancing and jumping.

(b) Emphasising changes of speed and effort.

## FLOORWORK

**Legs** (1) Seven linked moves with the emphasis on running the parts together, sometimes smoothly and almost gently, sometimes firmly and with strength. Balance; run; jump; land; lower; roll; rise. (2) Contrast, like variety and repetition, is included among the aesthetic qualities of sequences, and is to be encouraged.

**Body** (1) The whole body must be involved in the 'firm', wide, long, arched, twisted or curled balance. Feel the difference as you relax and move out of balance. (2) Many demonstrations and much teacher commentary are needed to extend the class repertoire of travelling on body parts into each new held balance position. Such travelling/linking is less well practised than travelling on feet or hands and feet.

**Arms** (1) The split, near horizontal legs help the balance and needs to be demonstrated in case the class does not understand. Pushing foot hardly leaves the floor. Leading, kicking up foot travels a long way past the upturned body. (2) Straight arms tend not to give and collapse like bent ones. Head faces forward, not back between hands which makes everything look upside down.

## APPARATUS WORK

**Ropes** Balanced start can be in contact with rope or not. Swing with hands together for strength. Land and roll. **Climbing frames** Balance can be with front, back or side towards frame, on seat, tummy, foot and hand, with many big body shapes. **Benches** Take-offs with one or both feet, with feet together or apart. Shape in flight a good contrast to final rolls. **Trestle** Balance on trestle, on trestle and floor, under trestle, on hands, hands and feet, seat, tummy, back, forearms. **Pyramid boxes and bench** Exciting, contrasting group. Be still; go; arrive and move along; fly; land and roll. **Boxes** Whole group must be aware of one another in action, even moving in and out of balance together, then changing to a new place for the next balance.

## FINAL FLOOR ACTIVITY

Emphasise that we are demonstrating contrast which is an important, eye catching feature in any sequence.

## LESSON PLAN • 30 MINUTES

### LESSON THEME

Direct teaching of simple gymnastic activities.

### FLOORWORK
16 minutes → **12 minutes**

**Legs** (1) Do a stretched upward jump on the spot. Land and bounce to half the height of the first jump. Repeat. Now do four full upward jumps. 'Jump and bounce, jump and bounce, jump, 2, 3, 4.' (2) Can you do all of that again, but this time plan to add some direction changes?

**Body** (1) Horizontal balance standing on one leg with upper body leaning forward to horizontal. Arms are stretched above head and other leg is stretched high behind so that arms, trunk and non-supporting leg make a long curving line. (2) Now lower to sitting in a 'V' position with legs straight and pointed upwards. Back is straight and arms help bal-ance. (3) Now rock back to shoulder balance with legs and body stretched up and vertical. Hands and arms press down on to floor to assist balanced stretch. (4) With a long swing of legs and rock of body, return to standing, then horizontal standing to repeat.

**Arms** (1) Bunny jumps on the spot. With hands flat on floor, arms straight, hips and shoulders are lifted to a position above hands by a push up from feet. Knees are bent. (2) Cat spring is like a travelling bunny jump to reach forward and support yourself on hands. From a crouched start, push whole body up and off floor a very short distance to land on hands with straight arms.

### APPARATUS WORK
**16 minutes**

**Ropes** Crossed feet grip. Try this from a standing position if strong enough, or from seated on a chair. Knees are apart and rope is gripped firmly under sole of one foot and above instep of other. Practise a small swing with arms straight, hands together. **Climbing frames** Start at bottom corner and climb up to top. Sit at top corner and come down diagonally, feet leading, to corner. **Mats** Forward rolls. Crouched start; hands on mat with head tucked in and chin on chest; push strongly with legs into roll keeping body tightly curled; heels come to floor near seat; reach forward to finish in crouched position, ready to go again. **Inverted benches** Stand astride bench, mount to balance standing, one foot in front of the other. **Low boxes** Bunny jump on to end of box. Cat spring along box top. Bunny jump to twist down from box. **Trestles, pyramid boxes** Downward circle on low pole. Body starts balanced on pole on top of thighs with a strong hand grip and well stretched body. Bend arms and hips to let waist rest on pole. Curl slowly round pole with *thumbs forward, fingers behind*, until knees come under pole. Lower feet quietly to floor.

### FINAL FLOOR ACTIVITY
**2 minutes**

Can you remember and repeat our opening jump, and do it once to each side of the room?

## NC requirements being emphasised

(a) Developing skill by exploring and making up activities.

(b) Trying hard to consolidate performance.

## FLOORWORK

**Legs** (1) Stretch everything in the air, particularly the ankle joints which are seldom fully extended in everyday life. 'Give' softly on landing. (2) They can travel to one side or other, forward or to rear, or they can make a quarter turn to face a different wall each time. **Body** (1) Strong work for back and shoulder muscles, as well as the one leg holding the balance. (2) Slow, controlled lower to sitting with difficult, straight arms, legs and spine, all working hard against sagging and giving. (3) Ask for 'Whose pointed feet and ankles are reaching up the highest towards the ceiling?' Body should be almost vertical over shoulders. (4) Strong arm swing and a bending of legs to tuck under you, are needed. **Arms** (1) 'Feel' strong with straight arms with hands pointing forwards for strength and efficiency. The ideal is to have hips above shoulders above hands, all in a vertical line. (2) In a cat spring, there is a moment when no body part is touching floor. The push up and forward comes from stretching the bent legs.

## APPARATUS WORK

**Ropes** A good test for crossed foot grip is to take one hand off the rope during the swing to see if you can retain your foot grip. **Climbing frames** Keep thumbs under the bars, fingers over, for a safe, strong grip. Try to spiral or rotate down to next bar. **Mats** Two rolls in succession allows 'end of one action to become the beginning of the next.' At end of each roll, emphasise one push with hands, not two, from floor. **Inverted benches** In the balance standing position you can practise standing on one foot and moving other foot back and forward, brushing side of bench before feeling for upper surface. This is how you feel your way forward, walking along the bench. **Low boxes** In bunny jumps you keep contact with floor. In cat springs there is a moment's flight with no contact with floor. **Trestles, pyramid boxes** Stress 'Thumbs forward' in circling down on pole, 'Head well in' in rolling forward on to mat from sitting, kneeling or a low crouch at pyramid boxes and their plank.

## FINAL FLOOR ACTIVITY

Jump and bounce; jump and bounce, jump, 2, 3, and turn.

## LESSON PLAN • 30 MINUTES

### LESSON THEME

Partner work to:

(a) make movements that you cannot do alone
(b) learn new activities from a partner
(c) recognise strengths and weaknesses of self and others and make allowances for them.

### FLOORWORK                                                    12 minutes

**Legs**
(1) Follow the leader who will vary the work by using different parts of the foot, varied directions and more than one body shape.
(2) New leader, can you take over and make your variety come from changing speed and adding on unusual arm and leg gestures?

**Body**
(1) In a stretching and curling sequence, can one partner do a full body stretch, with the other partner copying? Now the second partner leads into a curled shape, copied by the other partner. Continue stretching and curling, leading alternately.
(2) Can you work at different levels on a variety of supporting body parts?

**Arms**
(1) Partner A observes B going from feet to hands and back to feet, in two or three ways. A then tells B what was good in the demonstration and includes one teaching point to bring about improvement.
(2) After several repetitions, change duties.

### APPARATUS WORK                                               16 minutes

**Ropes**  Using ropes and mats, build up to a matching sequence, done together.

**Climbing frames**  Can you show me ways that you can travel over, under and around each other?

**Trestles, pole, planks**  Start at opposite ends of the apparatus. Approach and pass each other to finish in your partner's starting place.

**Bench, mats**  Build up to a matching sequence, in unison, starting from opposite sides. Include a flight.

**Boxes, mats, bench**  Lead and follow on the same pathway, using floor and apparatus, using similar or contrasting actions.

**Upturned bench, mats, boxes, plank**  Can you keep some contact with your partner as you balance, travel, balance?

### FINAL FLOOR ACTIVITY                                          2 minutes

Side by side, plan how you will run, jump and turn to face your starting place. Your turn can be in flight or on landing.

## NC requirements being emphasised

(a) Working safely, alone and with others.

(b) Exploring, improving and repeating a longer series of actions, making increasingly complex movement sequences.

(c) Making appropriate decisions quickly and planning responses.

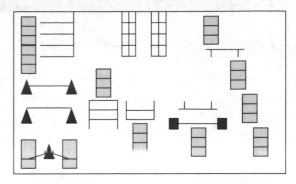

## FLOORWORK

**Legs** (1) Make the routine short enough to be able to remember and perform in unison. Follow at 2–3 metres so that follower can see actions and body shape clearly and easily. (2) New leader can develop existing routine with the change of speed and by addition of arm or leg gestures.

**Body** (1) Quick thinking and almost instant planning are needed to continue from partner's activity just seen. Keep going back to start to revise it, bit by bit. (2) High on feet; medium arched; low level stretching and curling travel of hands then feet.

**Arms** (1) Part complimentary observer, part coach and gentle critic, in the ideal one to one situation. (2) Observer looks for neatness with clear (not half-hearted) shapes, well-controlled, safe, strong arm work, obvious starting and finishing positions, and something original and personal about it.

## APPARATUS WORK

**Ropes** Plan, practise and build up your beginning, middle and end step by step. **Climbing frames** One can be stationary, one travelling; or they can continually be meeting and passing, on same or opposite sides. **Trestles** An exercise in 'negotiating' an obstacle, your partner, ideally with no contact. **Bench, mats** Decide on a starting signal, such as a heel raising by one. Check approach action, action and shape from bench, and the finish, landing in balance or rolling to a finish. **Boxes, bench** Leader goes and waits. Partner follows. This gives time to note the actions, shapes, directions for partner to match or to contrast. **Upturned bench, boxes, plank** Contact can be made by side by side travel, or one walking backwards holding other, or an assisted jump or lift.

## FINAL FLOOR ACTIVITY

With a light hand hold at shoulder level, they can run side by side into a jump with a swing up of the same leg to twist to face where they came from. As they land, gently and slowly, side by side, the other hand can be joined at shoulder level, for the return to their starting places.

## LESSON PLAN • 30–35 MINUTES

At the start of the year the lesson's main emphases include:

(a) creating a safe, caring, quiet atmosphere where all co-operate sensibly and unselfishly, particularly in sharing space
(b) establishing a tradition of immediate responses to instructions
(c) establishing a tradition of lessons being filled with vigorous, wholehearted, physical activity.

## FLOORWORK                                                    12–15 minutes

**Legs** (1) Show me your best running, keeping well away from others. (2) When I call 'Stop!' move quickly into your own space and show me a tall, stretched balance on tip toes. Stop! (Repeat.) (3) Good running is quiet and you don't follow anyone. Visit all parts of the room and run on straight lines, not curves. (4) Lift heels, knees, arms and chest to make your running quiet and neat. Stop! (Well spaced, stretched on tip toes.)
**Body** (1) Lie on your back, curled up tightly, with hands clasped under knees. Can you roll, slowly, from side to side? (2) Still curled up tightly, can you roll forward and back on to shoulders and hands? Practise the strong hand push to stop the roll back and to start the roll forward.
**Arms** (1) Slowly, and keeping well away from others, show me ways that you can travel, using feet and hands. (2) Can you try movements using hands only, then feet only? (3) Can you vary your travelling by having front, back or side to the floor, or be upended, as in cartwheels?

## APPARATUS WORK                                              16–18 minutes

(1) Travel to all parts of the room, going in and out, along, across, and under apparatus, touching only mats and floor to start with.
(2) When I call 'Stop!' quickly show me a fully stretched body on the nearest piece of apparatus. Stop! (Repeat.)
(3) Travel up to, on and away from pieces of apparatus, using feet only. Use your feet well on floor and apparatus and show me how sensibly you are sharing space with others.
(4) Travel on floor and apparatus, using feet and hands only.

(5) Stay at your present group of apparatus to repeat, practise and improve the following. (a) Start and finish away from the apparatus in a floor space. (b) Include neat travelling on feet, and hands and feet. (c) Rolling on mats, on apparatus or from apparatus. (d) At some point, which could be the very beginning or end, show me a beautifully stretched, still body.

## FINAL FLOOR ACTIVITY                                           2 minutes

Start in a tall, still starting position. Run quietly and well, to visit all parts of the room, the sides, corners, ends and the middle. Run on straight lines and do not follow anyone.

## NC requirements being emphasised
(a) Being taught to be physically active.
(b) Responding readily to instructions.

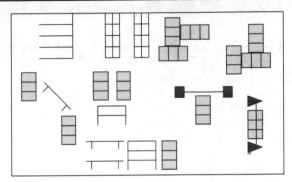

## FLOORWORK

**Legs** (1) Discourage any tendency to anti-clockwise running, all following one another in a big circle, common in primary schools. (2) 'Stop!' is an exercise in 'responding readily to instructions', an essential tradition, to be established every September. (3) Demonstrate with those who move along straight lines, looking out for and keeping well away from others. (4) Demonstrate with and praise those whose running appears to be lifting up off the floor, as they travel so lightly.

**Body** (1) The rocking starts with a swing to one side with hands and knees. Chin is on chest, keeping back rounded and easy to roll on. (2) For the roll back and forward, hands are placed beside shoulders with thumb in and small finger out, with elbows lifted high. Going back is like the start of a backward roll. Going forward, helped by the strong hands push, is like the end of a forward roll.

**Arms** (1) Insist on slow, thoughtful actions, not quick, untidy scampering. (2) Hands only, then feet only adventurous handwalking and cartwheels, or an easy crawling action, walking forward on hands as far as you can go, then walking feet up beside hands again. (3) Challenge them to vary the leading body parts (not always the head) and not always to have front towards floor.

## APPARATUS WORK

(1) This is an exercise in travelling on the floor, in a variety of ways, between apparatus. During apparatus work, the floor travelling is often ignored in favour of that on apparatus. (2) 'Stop!' demands an instant response on the nearest piece of apparatus, and requires them to listen, while they are travelling. Praise those whose stretched body is on a part other than the easy feet or feet and hands. (3) Pursue vigour and wholehearted, non-stop activity. Use eyes to see a space. Wait your turn in coming from apparatus on to the mats.

Because it is feet only travelling, the ropes and frames are not included yet. Look out for and identify walking, running, jumping, bouncing, skipping, balancing, springing, hopscotching. (4) Much commenting by the circulating teacher, praising the wide variety of responses seen, helps expand the class repertoire. (5) *Plan* your travelling, rolling and balance. *Perform* it after much repetition, improving and remembering. *Reflect* after each performance, then adapt as necessary to bring about improvement.

## FINAL FLOOR ACTIVITY

If they pretend to have chalk on their feet, they should leave their mark in corners, sides, ends.

## LESSON PLAN • 30–35 MINUTES

The lesson's main emphasis is on developing a tradition of quiet, continuous work with an awareness of the need for good spacing. The equally desirable tradition of wholehearted participation means working the body strongly and using the full range of movement possible in the joints concerned.

### FLOORWORK                                    12–15 minutes

**Legs** (1) Join together a short walk, a short run and a vigorous high jump. Land quietly, using your arms to balance you, and be still. Look for a space and continue. (2) In your high jump, stretch every part of your body, with arms reaching up and toes and ankles stretched down. (3) Think of making a 'squashy' landing with knees giving to make a soft, quiet action.

**Body** Balancing means that your body is on some small or unusual part or parts and wanting to 'wobble'. (1) Show me an easy balance on one foot. Stretch strongly the leg and arms not being used to make your body work hard. (2) Move to some other part or parts and show me a new balance. Once again, stretch hard the parts not being used. (3) Keep working at three or four different balances. Each time hold the position strongly. The stretching of non-supporting parts makes you work really hard and makes your balance position look more attractive and 'gymnastic'.

**Arms** (1) Keep your body in the crouched 'bunny jump' position with bent legs and straight arms. Keep your fingers spread with hands pointing forward and travel in and out of the others. (2) Can you lift your 'bunny jump' high enough to place your shoulders over your hips over your hands?

### APPARATUS WORK                               16–18 minutes

(1) Travel to different pieces of apparatus and find ways to move on them. Can you leave with a high jump and soft landing?

(2) Start and finish away from each piece of apparatus. Show me your ways of travelling on floor and apparatus. Include movements using legs, arms, and can you show me a still, stretched balance?

(3) Go from apparatus to apparatus, showing me a 'bunny jump' action on each with straight arms and bent legs.

(4) Stay at your present piece of apparatus in small groups of about five to practise, repeat and improve the following.

(a) Start and finish away from the apparatus.
(b) Show varied ways of travelling up to it using legs.
(c) Make your hands important in travelling on the apparatus, trying at some point to take all the weight on your hands.
(d) At some point hold a beautifully still, stretched balance.

### FINAL FLOOR ACTIVITY                          2 minutes

Walking, running and long jumping, travel to all parts of the room.

## NC requirements being emphasised

(**a**) Exploring different means of jumping, balancing and taking weight on hands.

(**b**) Improving and repeating longer and increasingly complex sequences of movement.

## FLOORWORK

**Legs** (**1**) A 3–4 metre line is long enough to include all three actions. The strength felt in the vigorous spring upwards should also be felt in the stretched body in its flight. (**2**) A full, clear body shape contributes to the appearance and the 'correctness' in a performance, and proves we are working hard. (**3**) Absorbing impact by a 'giving' in the knees and ankles becomes even more important from apparatus.

**Body** (**1**) In balancing, encourage them to stretch the body parts not supporting the body, to work harder and look better. No sagging! (**2**) Moving to an adjacent body part for support requires careful rolling, sitting, rocking, lowering, twisting, arching, levering.

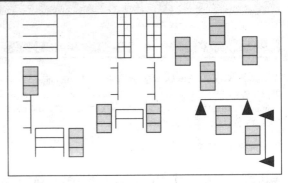

(**3**) Demonstrations by groups of good performers will help to swell the class repertoire in this difficult activity. Some might even work hard to hold a still handstand for two or three seconds.

**Arms** (**1**) The bunny jump travelling can be made more interesting by a twisting, zig zag pathway, side to side, over a line. (**2**) Two or three preliminary bounces on the hands can be done. 'Bounce, bounce, bounce and spring up!'

## APPARATUS WORK

(**1**) Teacher's commentary on the many actions being seen helps to spread ideas – climbing, swinging, rolling, sliding, pulling, vaulting, circling, hanging, balancing. Praise should be given for good high jumps up to and from apparatus. (**2**) Remember that hands and feet can support you on the floor in addition to the feet only, more commonly seen. The still, stretched balance could be the start or finish position, on toes away from the apparatus, or a held position on the apparatus. (**3**) Class can be asked to 'Show me your hands', hands held towards teacher to show straight arms with fingers pointing forward. This strong, safe hand and arm position is now used. Going from apparatus to apparatus, with a high spring up to a bunny jump. (**4**) *Plan* for variety in leg travelling; varied uses and grips by hands; all weight on hands, carefully; and a whole body, stretched balance at some point – start, middle or finish. *Reflect*, then think about and *plan* how to alter it to improve it. *Perform* even better work.

## FINAL FLOOR ACTIVITY

Short walk, short run, jump, with the jump the main part to be demonstrated, using all parts of the room.

## LESSON PLAN • 30–35 MINUTES

The lesson's emphasis is on developing quality and variety in the many natural body activities that children experience in a lively, varied, gymnastics lesson. As the term implies 'natural body activities' includes all forms of travelling, jumping, landing, rolling, swinging, climbing, balancing and hanging.

### FLOORWORK                                                           12–15 minutes

**Legs** (1) As you travel to all parts of the room, using legs only, can you include two or three different actions, performed quietly, neatly, and with an obvious contrast somewhere (e.g. quiet tip toe walking; easy skipping with a full arm swing; and a vigorous upward jump)? (2) Remember that your travelling actions are good when they are neat, quiet and not following anyone. Travel on straight lines which means that you have to keep changing direction, not on a curve where everyone is following everyone.

**Body** (1) Experiment with different actions you can do while you travel on a variety of body parts. (2) If you start off, *balanced*, say, on one foot or one foot and one hand, can you *lower* to a larger body part such as shoulders or seat; then can you *roll* on to, for example, knees and elbows; then *swing up* to start all over again?

**Arms** (1) Show me some of the ways that you can plan to go from feet only, to being on hands only, to returning to feet only. (2) On the spot can you include handstands and bunny jumps? Low travels can be springs from low crouch on to hands; high travels can include cartwheels and handwalking.

### APPARATUS WORK                                                      16–18 minutes

(1) Travel to all parts of the room, touching floor and mats only. Make your actions fit the spaces and the obstacles that you meet, using legs only (e.g. walk, run or skip on open floor; roll or leap across mats; spring or cartwheel over benches; step through spaces in frames; bounce, feet astride, along benches).

(2) Now change to travelling on apparatus and floor and, once again let your many actions fit the places where you are travelling (e.g. swing on a rope; spring off a bench; cartwheel or roll across a mat; vault over a box or bench; balance on a bench; hang on a bar or rope; circle on a rope or bar).

(3) Stay at your present group of apparatus in small groups to practise, repeat and improve the following. (a) Start and finish, in own floor space in a still, 'firm' position. (b) Plan to include a variety of natural actions to take you up to, on, along and away from the apparatus. Make these actions fit the places and the spaces where you are working. (c) Can you include some travelling on feet only; on different body parts; and on hands and feet, as we practised in our floorwork?

### FINAL FLOOR ACTIVITY                                                2 minutes

Using feet only, travel to every part of the room using movements where your feet stay near to the floor as they travel.

## NC requirements being emphasised

(a) Making appropriate decisions quickly and planning their responses.

(b) Making judgements of performances and suggesting ways to improve.

## FLOORWORK

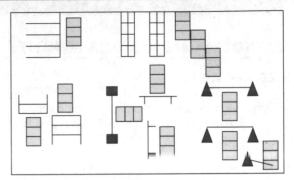

**Legs** (1) 'Contrast' comes from changes of effort (e.g. vigorous or gentle actions, firm or relaxed body) and speed used (slow, normal, accelerating or quick). The 'How?' (2) Thinking about the 'Where?', the straight line travelling is asked for to counter any tendency to the anti-clockwise travel in a big circle, common in primary schools, with all following all.

**Body** (1) Travelling on a variety of body parts, ideally, will include at least three examples as a good challenge. For example, a run into a jump, land, lower on to back, roll sideways right over on to front, stand and then cartwheel. (2) The example given can be offered to those who are less 'creative' to get them started quickly, and to give them something to develop and adapt as their own.

**Arms** (1) Emphasise 'Feet only on to hands only', not feet and hands. It sometimes helps to pretend that you are working on to, across or along a bench from a starting position on the floor. (2) Once again, direct teaching as in the previous, body activity, can give them all a varied sequence to practise, and then develop in their own way.

## APPARATUS WORK

(1) Quick reactions ('making appropriate decisions quickly') are needed to fit the actions to the small, large, wide or narrow spaces encountered. (2) Similar fitting of actions to spaces, but this time on floor and on apparatus. Plan to include actions that use hands, hands and feet, feet, and other large body parts for variety. Plan to use just the right amount of effort for a controlled, quality performance. (3) A sequence of natural actions, staying at a group of apparatus with four or five others only, to enable you to practise, repeat, remember and improve. *Plan* for variety and quality with a definite beginning, middle and end. *Perform* wholeheartedly to improve. *Reflect and evaluate*, adapt, practise, improve and remember.

## FINAL FLOOR ACTIVITY

Walking, low skipping, running 'skimming' the floor, slipping sideways (low chasse).

## LESSON PLAN • 30–35 MINUTES

### LESSON THEME

Body parts awareness and learning to 'feel' and understand how the body works and moves in its many ways to support, receive and transfer body weight.

### FLOORWORK                                    12–15 minutes

**Legs** (1) Practise soft, quiet upward jumps on the spot. Really stretch the ankles at take-off, and let them 'give' on landing. Feel the firm stretch in your whole body going up. Feel the gentle 'give' in ankles and knees on landing.   (2) Skip round the room using the same good stretch in the pushing ankle. Let the opposite leg bend high forwards with its ankle well stretched and the opposite arm reach forward as a balance. (Opposite arm and thigh horizontal.)

**Body** Stand with feet apart. Slowly bend down leading with your head. Neck joints, shoulders, back, waist, hips, knees and ankles all 'give' until you are crouched on two feet. Now rise up in the opposite order, stretching ankles, knees, hips, waist, back, shoulders, neck and finish by stretching arms high above head. Lower arms and repeat, feeling the exact order in which the joints close and open.

**Arms** Travel slowly on hands and feet, in and out of the others. Try keeping arms and legs straight, together or apart for a very strong movement. You can move arms only, then legs only; or left side, then right side; or opposite as in crawling. A really strong action is bouncing along, springing everything up off the floor.

### APPARATUS WORK                                16–18 minutes

(1) Walk, run, jump or skip round all the apparatus, touching only the floor and the mats. When I call 'Stop!' quickly find a place on the nearest piece of apparatus, with both feet off the apparatus and ankles stretched strongly. Stop! (Repeat.)

(2) When I stop you next time, show me a fully stretched body on a piece of apparatus. Stop! Now, slowly curl into a rounded shape.

(3) Next time, can you be stretched on a different body part on a different piece of apparatus? Stop! Slowly curl everything in.

(4) Walk to many pieces of apparatus and try out the ways your hands can lift, lever, jump, circle, twist you on to apparatus.

(5) Stay at your present set of apparatus, in small groups of five or six to work hard at the following activities to feel how our different body parts work to receive, support and transfer our weight on, across, under, around, along and from the varied apparatus. **Mats** Rolling. **Climbing frames** Climbing. **Ropes** Swinging or climbing. **Trestles, poles, planks** Travelling. **Inverted benches, trestle** Balancing. **Boxes, mats, bench** Running and jumping; rolling; weight on hands.

### FINAL FLOOR ACTIVITY                                2 minutes

Can you make different parts of your body lead in your travelling (knees, head, elbow, etc.)?

## NC requirements being emphasised

(a) Developing skill by exploring and making up activities and by expressing themselves imaginatively.

(b) Sustaining energetic activity and showing an understanding of what happens to the body during exercise.

## FLOORWORK

**Legs** (1) The ankle joint is seldom fully stretched in everyday life and is often stiff and weak. Demonstrate with strong, supple pupils to show the strong downward stretch and drive at take-off, and the soft, controlled, 'give' in ankles on landing. (2) The stretch in both the take-off ankle and the one high ahead on leading leg is looked for here. The one driving foot and ankle have to work hard to propel the whole body weight, and the one receiving foot and ankle work hard to receive and support all the body weight.

**Body** Teacher can talk them down, joint by joint. Class can talk through the opposite actions. 'Unroll ankles, knees, hips, waist, lower, middle, upper back, neck, shoulders, elbows, wrists to full stretch.'

**Arms** By travelling slowly and using body parts to their fullest movement, we are able to recognise the actions, and we are working our bodies strongly. Quick scampering with most weight on feet is neither attractive to look at, or good exercise.

## APPARATUS WORK

(1) 'Feet and ankles off apparatus' ensures an interesting position on a variety of other body parts. (Seat, front, back, side, shoulders.) (2) They have to plan a stopping position where they are fully stretched, and from which they are able to curl slowly. (3) Demonstrations at the previous activity should extend the range presented here. (4) They are thinking 'Hands' and trying to name the many actions possible in lifting us on to, across, around, along, under, up and down apparatus. (5) **Mats** Feel chin on chest going forward, shoulders contacting first (not head) and feel heels close to seat before standing. **Climbing frames** Thumbs under the bars, fingers on top for all climbing, for a strong, safe grip. **Ropes** Hands together for a strong grip for swinging or to start the climb as you lift both feet. **Inverted benches, trestle** Balance on small or unusual body parts, or small or unusual apparatus surfaces, without wobbling. **Trestles** Remain on for most of the time as you travel under, along, around, across with as many grips as possible. **Boxes, plank, bench** Excellent contrast in body actions – lively run and jump; smooth, easy rolls; and a moment's stillness on hands.

## FINAL FLOOR ACTIVITY

Ask 'How many body parts can you lead with in the next two minutes? Count as you go.'

## LESSON PLAN • 30–35 MINUTES

### LESSON THEME

Body shape awareness in held positions and on the move. Awareness of long, wide, curled or twisted body shapes within own performances and those of others. Shape's contribution to good style and to efficiency of movements.

### FLOORWORK                                                    12–15 minutes

**Legs** Stand tall and ready to go with all parts of your body stretched strongly. Run and jump with a long, then a wide, then a tucked body shape in flight. Let your knees 'give' for a quiet, soft landing, but keep your upper body straight for a good balanced finish. Stretched arms for balance can be forward, above head or sideways.

**Body** Using different starting positions, can you change from one wide body shape to another (e.g. from standing, feet and arms stretched wide; to front support position on floor, spread wide; to side falling on one foot and one hand, body side on to floor with upper arm and leg stretched to make a wide shape; to back lying, stretched wide; to balanced on shoulders, feet wide, etc.)?

**Arms** (1) With hands on floor, can you jump your feet in the air, kicking them strongly and keeping them stretched (kicking horses)? (2) Practise 'bunny jumps' on two hands with legs kept curled.

### APPARATUS WORK                                              16–18 minutes

(1) As you travel all round the room on floor and mats only, can you emphasise your body shape? For example, very straight or well bent arms and legs in your walking or running; or bounding along on two feet, wide or lifting into a tuck.

(2) When I call 'Stop!' quickly find a place on the nearest apparatus where you can balance, hang or support yourself and show me a clear body shape. Stop! (Repeat.)

(3) Travel, using all apparatus and find a variety of places on, under, round, across, hanging where you can show me a variety of body shapes which make your held position look neat and which are quite difficult to hold.

(4) In your small groups of five or six, start at your present set of apparatus to repeat, improve and be able to demonstrate the following. (a) Start away from apparatus; travel up to, on and away from the apparatus to finish in your own floor space, and include . . . (b) Travelling through contrasting shapes (e.g. rolls contrasting with stretched and wide jumps; rolling into a wide balance; twisting on and stretching along, etc.). Remember to include poised and still starting and finishing positions which do not always have to be on feet.

### FINAL FLOOR ACTIVITY                                        2 minutes

Show me a triangle of three jumps to bring you back to your starting place. Include three different shapes in the air.

## NC requirements being emphasised

(a) Emphasising changes of shape through gymnastic actions.
(b) Adopting good posture and the appropriate use of the body.

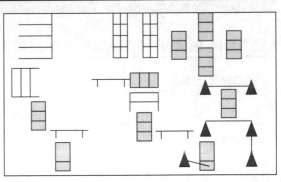

## FLOORWORK

**Legs** Use a short, 3–4-metre run only, since the jump is the main activity. Performing on a triangle helps to provide a repeating start and finish place. Body shape interest is widespread – erect body at start, three, whole body shapes in flight, and good use of stretched arms for balance in flight and on landing.

**Body** To help them into action in this difficult challenge, a series of three or four positions with their linking actions can be suggested and/or led by the teacher. During the following weeks they will adapt and develop their own series.

**Arms** (1) Arms and legs are strongly stretched in the kicking horses. Straight arms are strong and do not tend to give as slightly bent arms do. The kicking action, front to rear, seems to assist and keep putting the body into balance. (2) Bent legs are short levers and bounce up into the bunny jump position more easily and quickly than straighter legs. Two or three, preliminary little bounces of feet up and off floor, are a help as you gather for the strong bounce up and on to hands. They aim to place hips above shoulders above hands, all in a line.

## APPARATUS WORK

(1) No action can be done without a body shape. Be aware of the shape and work hard to make it full and firm. Remember that it always looks better, and is more efficient and correct, when the shape is right. (2) Stop and respond immediately, to show a clear, whole body shape on the nearest piece of apparatus. If there is a body part not touching the apparatus or supporting you, stretch it firmly away, to enhance the appearance of the performance. (3) More leisurely travelling, now, to visit all apparatus in turn to show varied, still body shapes (e.g. stretched hanging from a bar of climbing frame; curled hanging from two ropes; curled round a metal pole; back arched on a mat; wide, side on to a climbing frame, holding with one hand and one foot). (4) *Plan*: (a) your pathway from start to finish (b) your choice of actions that highlight changing shape while travelling. *Perform* two or three times to improve. *Reflect*, adapt, repeat, improve, remember.

## FINAL FLOOR ACTIVITY

Discourage long-sided triangles. A 3-metre side is sufficient because the jumps, not the runs, are the main parts. What shapes? What take-off and landing actions?

## LESSON PLAN • 30–35 MINUTES

### LESSON THEME

Direct teaching of simple, safe Gymnastic Activities.

### FLOORWORK                                                    12 minutes

**Legs** (1) Skip jumping on the spot with good stretch in ankles at take-off, and a soft 'give' on landing. Do four to each side of room. (2) Three skip jumps on the spot and a tucked jump (knees high, lifted to chest) on four. Turn to face next wall and repeat. (3) Can you continue this activity and add your own jump on count of four, e.g. tuck, jacknife, star, twist with heels up and back to one side?
**Body** (1) Roll to face opposite way. Sit with feet wide apart and arms straight and down by sides. Lean over, straight to one side, on to back, with legs still wide and straight, poin-ting up. Now complete turn by swinging leg down to floor and pulling body up to a seated position again, legs still wide and straight. (2) Now, can you do it all the way back to where you began?
**Arms** Cartwheels. An easy introduction is to ask class to pretend that they are standing on a big hoop, with feet apart. One hand reaches down on to another part of hoop, feet push off and second hand touches down further round the hoop, then feet return to hoop, one after the other, with twist of body.

### APPARATUS WORK                                              18 minutes

**Mats** Revise cartwheels. Try a backward roll from sitting, heel close to seat, hands up above shoulders, thumbs near to ears. Back is rounded and chin is on chest. Roll back on to flat hands on floor, thumbs still near ears.
**Upturned benches and mats** Balance walk forwards. From balanced standing on bench, the leading foot feels its way alongside the supporting surface. The foot carefully feels for the balance surface before putting weight down. **Ropes** Try swinging with hands together and feet crossed on the rope. A strong foot grip means that you can take one hand away without sliding off rope. **Cross** **low boxes** Face vault is a bunny jump over the box. You approach at right angles, and place hands obliquely on box. With a two-footed take-off, spring up and over the box, seat well up and over hands, and knees bent. You face the box all the way across. **Climbing frames** Travel by moving the feet by themselves, then the hands by themselves. Can you do this in a rectangle of 4–6 spaces? **Trestles, pole, planks** Show me those parts of the apparatus where you can hang, using hands only, hands and feet, hands and one leg, tummy, backs of knees. Can you hang and stretch, hang and curl?

### FINAL FLOOR ACTIVITY                                         2 minutes

Can you do four skip jumps on the spot, then do four little ones travelling forward, then four to one side, then four straight back, then four to one side to finish where you started?

## NC requirements being emphasised

(a) Exploring different means of rolling, swinging, jumping and taking weight on hands.

(b) Developing their skill by exploring and making up activities.

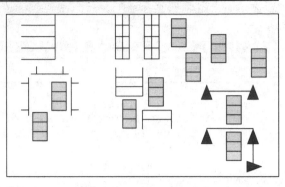

## FLOORWORK

**Legs** (1) A full, strong stretching in the ankle joint at take-off, and a silent, soft 'give' in the ankles on landing, are the main features to start with. (2) Good height is needed to give you time to add the tucked position. (3) Look out for, praise and demonstrate with those whose big effort is producing sufficient height to do a clear, firm and impressive shape, followed by a beautifully quiet, controlled landing.

**Body** (1) Circle roll is a favourite way to change direction. For example, forward roll to straddle sitting. Circle roll back to face your starting position. (2) Class perform to circle roll away from the teacher to face the opposite wall, then perform to come back to starting place again.

**Arms** Cartwheels can be low and almost circular for learners, progressing to a straight line for more capable performers.

## APPARATUS WORK

**Mats** Cartwheel with greater comfort on a mat. 'Hand, push off to other hand, foot, foot.'

**Upturned benches** Stand astride bench. Mount to balance standing. Do not look down. Feel your way along balance surface, keeping contact with some part of both feet. The walking forward can be enhanced by a high knee raising of non-supporting leg. You can also balance walk backwards and sideways. **Ropes** Hands together means hands are both working strongly during swings. On a climb, reach up with one hand, then other hand, then first hand next to second hand for the hands together pull. **Cross low boxes** High bunny jumps become face vaults across box. Legs are kept bent, arms are straight and you twist round and off, facing box all the time. **Climbing frames** There will be much stretching and curling as you travel, hands only, feet only. When hand grip is used, stress 'Fingers grip over one side away from you, thumbs grip under and towards you.' **Trestles** A 'gripping' activity, full of variety which will deserve to be demonstrated to increase the class and the teacher's repertoire.

## FINAL FLOOR ACTIVITY

A set of 20 jumps as a whole class activity, performed slowly and softly, is a pleasing ending.

## LESSON PLAN • 30–35 MINUTES

### LESSON THEME

Space awareness and understanding the 'where' of movement as we share the floor and apparatus with others moving vigorously. The variety and quality of the work is improved by good and varied use of directions, levels and pathways and by understanding the difference between own space and general space.

### FLOORWORK                                                    12–15 minutes

**Legs** Travel using your legs and include different directions. Can you show me which actions travel easily in sideways or backward directions, and which most easily in a forward direction (e.g. chasse or slip step sideways, small skipping steps backwards)?

**Body** With your body in a bridge-like shape, can you travel in different directions (e.g. forwards, backwards, sideways on hands and feet, with front, back or side towards the floor)?

**Arms** Experiment with one, two or alternate hands supporting you. Can you take your legs up into the air space above your head then bring them down in a new space on the floor (e.g. low 'bunny jumps' across a line or high cartwheels along a line)?

### APPARATUS WORK                                               16–18 minutes

(1) Show me a lively leg activity in your own personal space. Then travel on floor and apparatus, occasionally changing directions, up to, on or from the apparatus to a new own space to start again.

(2) Can you approach apparatus facing forwards and leave it facing sideways or, very carefully, backwards?

(3) Stay at your own starting group places in fives or sixes to practise, improve and remember the following. **Mats** Can you plan and practise a sequence of three or four bridge-like shapes with the emphasis on changing levels? **Climbing frames** Can you travel, using a small group of 4–6 spaces, then travel using the whole frame? Plan to let different parts of your body lead. **Ropes, benches, mats** As you swing can you demonstrate direction changes? Your swing can start from mat, bench or after a short run and you can swing by jumping on to a swinging rope. **Trestles, poles, planks** All stay on the apparatus, sharing it sensibly as you travel along, across, around, or under, sometimes with your body very near or well away from the apparatus. **Long bench, mat, cross bench, mat** Zig-zag along the long bench and mat. At the return cross bench, show me a running high jump. **Boxes, mats** Arrive on the apparatus facing forward. Leave facing another way.

### FINAL FLOOR ACTIVITY                                         2 minutes

Run with four easy actions, then four with high knees in your own floor space. Then run normally all round the room and back to your own floor space.

# LESSON NOTES • 4–5 LESSONS DEVELOPMENT

## NC requirements being emphasised

(a) Changes of direction and level to be emphasised through gymnastic actions.
(b) Practising, adapting, improving and repeating longer and more complex sequences of movement.

## FLOORWORK

**Legs** Establish good use of space to practise and to avoid impeding others. Going backwards needs to be slow and careful, looking back over one shoulder. A triangular pathway uses space well (e.g. forward, then sideways, then backwards to starting place).
**Body** Very easy travel on feet with body arched forward, back or to one side. Quite easy travel on hand and feet. Difficult travel, walking on hands with arch below knees.
**Arms** One-handed twisting, low bunny jumps. Two-handed, high bunny jumps. Handstands. Alternate hands cartwheels.

## APPARATUS WORK

(1) Focus on 'My space and whole room space, and direction changes.' (2) While we want virtually non-stop activity, we should sometimes wait until there is plenty of space before leaving apparatus, sideways or backwards, for our own and others' safety. (3) **Mats** 'Bridging' can include sitting (bridge under knees); side falling on one hand and one foot; face down on hands and feet, or on knees and elbows; arched with back to floor on hands and feet, or on shoulders and feet; standing arched forward, sideways or to rear.
**Climbing frames** You can weave in and out of small groups of spaces with hands, head or feet leading. In using the whole frame, you can lead up with head, to side with one side, down with feet. **Ropes, bench, mats** Change direction in flight, on landing, after landing.
**Trestles, poles, mats** Group activity with non-stop action, sharing apparatus and floor beneath. Try to plan pathway from floor start to floor finish. Include some under, on, around, across for variety. **Benches, mats** Zig-zag travel can be on one or both hands, side to side; feet together or alternate; both hands and feet; on to and from (e.g. bunny jumps, cat springs); starting beside or further away from bench; across without touching.
**Boxes, mats** Much teacher commentary to accompany the actions on (roll, cat spring, jump, bunny jump, step, swing of leg or arm) and off (sideways or carefully backwards, stepping, jumping, rolling).

## FINAL FLOOR ACTIVITY

A three part activity. Run into a space near you, taking four counts to arrive. Run on the spot with four sets of high knee liftings. Run, using a lot of room space, back to your own starting place to finish, standing still. Repeat.

## LESSON PLAN • 30–35 MINUTES

### LESSON THEME

Balance and some of the ways in which the body can move into, hold and move from balanced stillness.

### FLOORWORK                                                    12–15 minutes

**Legs** Stand, balanced and stretched tall, on tip toes with arms and heels high, or even on one foot only. Use a short run into a good space, jump up high and land, beautifully balanced. Use stretched arms strongly to help control in the air, and on landing. Experiment with feet positions on landing to give you easy balance. (Jumping into balance.)

**Body** Can you hold your body in balance on three different bases, and can you make the body shape different with each balance? See if rolls can help you to link your balances together. For example, star shape on one foot; lower and roll up into a long stretch on shoulders; roll back over one shoulder into a bridge on hands and tip toes.

**Arms** Teach elbow balance. From a crouch position with feet apart, place hands on floor, shoulder width apart and under shoulders. Bend elbows slightly to place them inside and under knees. Tilt body forward slowly, from feet on to hands, until toes come a short distance off the floor, and you are balancing on hands only. (Tilting into balance.)

### APPARATUS WORK                                              16–18 minutes

(1) Travel freely from apparatus to apparatus and show me a still balance on each, using different body parts to support you. Plan also to try to include different methods of moving into your held position. You can jump, roll, swing, twist or lever.

(2) Stay at your own starting group places to practise, improve, repeat and remember the following. **Ropes** Can you swing, let go at end of swing and land in a good balance position? **Boxes, mats, trestles** As a whole group, demonstrate a variety of balances and try to include a variety of levels, supporting parts and body shapes. **Inverted benches, mats** Balance walk forward on bench, keeping some part of both feet touching the bench at all times. On the mats, can you balance, roll, balance? **Climbing frames** Follow your leader, travelling and holding still balances all over the frame. **Low box, bench, mats** Use the apparatus as spring boards from which to do an explosive high jump, followed by a beautifully controlled and balanced landing. **Mats** Show your partner your floorwork sequence of three balances with changing body shapes. Your partner will help you by suggesting one way in which to make an improvement.

### FINAL FLOOR ACTIVITY                                        2 minutes

Jump up on the spot and land in excellent balance; run a short distance and land, well controlled in a good 'firm' balance.

## NC requirements being emphasised

(a) Balancing, both on floor and apparatus.
(b) Adopting good posture and the appropriate use of the body.

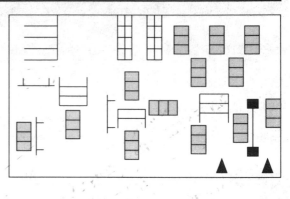

## FLOORWORK

**Legs** Balance is helped by landing with one foot after the other and keeping feet apart. This 'One . . . two' controlled, quite slow landing helps produce a nicely balanced finish. Stretched arms forwards or sideways also help balance and make the movement look good and 'gymnastic.'

**Body** A contrast between the static, held balance and the rolling, rocking, tilting, levering, moving link movements is to be encouraged.

**Arms** If elbow balance is too difficult, ask for a 'two count bunny jump', trying to hold it for two seconds with straight arms under shoulders under hips, and knees well bent to keep centre of gravity low.

## APPARATUS WORK

(1) 'Can you visit all six different sets of apparatus, and each time, balance on a different part or parts of your body? (2) **Ropes** Build up to letting go by holding on and landing, to start with. Then let go with one hand, and finally, both hands. **Boxes, mats, trestles** Group activity which looks particularly good when all move into, hold and move out of balance together. **Inverted benches, mats** 'Feel for bench. No looking down. Keep part of both feet in contact with the balance bench.'

**Climbing frames** Note your leader's actions, body parts involved in travelling. In the balances, look out for body parts supporting and the clear body shape held. **Low box, bench, mats** Explosive high jumps can be after run or from standing on box or bench. Show good body tension to land firm and under control, with no wobbling. **Mats** Teaching partner will remember to 'Teach only one improvement at a time.'

## FINAL FLOOR ACTIVITY

Jump on the spot will be from both feet to both feet. The jump after the short run can be from one foot or both feet to one foot after the other, or to both feet together or apart.

## LESSON PLAN • 30–35 MINUTES

### LESSON THEME

Swinging as an impetus and aid to movement.

### FLOORWORK                                             12–15 minutes

**Legs** (1) Practise swinging into an upward jump on the spot with a long pull upward of the arms. Including arms above head, stretch everything strongly. (2) Let ankles stretch strongly in the air and 'give' for a soft, quiet landing. (3) Change to a soft run into a strong swing into an upward jump. (With arm and/or leg.) (4) Now show me a swing into your upward jump on the spot, then your short run and swing into an upward jump. Land, well balanced, helped by arms stretched forward or sideways.
**Body** (1) Sitting, curled up small, can you roll back and forward? Swing back on to hands and shoulders with your upper body.

Swing forward to curled up sitting with a long swing of your legs. (Long straight legs give excellent swing.) (2) Can you roll from side to side on your back, curled up small? The swing will come from the arms and legs. (3) Can you swing left, then right, then a big swing to left and right over on to front and on to back again? Keep curled up small, with head on to knees.
**Arms** Starting with arms above head can you try a long, slow swing up into handstand? After a few practices, try the quicker, shorter swing up with one leg. To help your balance on hands, try to make a straight line with your legs, like a tight rope walker's pole.

### APPARATUS WORK                                         16–18 minutes

(1) Travel on floor and mats only. Can you show me swings into jumps on the floor, across mats or over low apparatus?
(2) When you come to a mat, can you swing into a forward, sideways or backward roll?
(3) Supporting your body on hands only, can you swing legs off the floor? Bent legs are easier to lift than straight ones.
(4) Can you swing arms and/or a leg to bring you on to apparatus? Swing up and off with a stretched jump and a nice, squashy landing.

(5) Stay at your starting group place in fives or sixes to repeat, practise, improve and remember the following. (**a**) Start and finish on the floor away from the apparatus. Travel up to, on, along and away from the apparatus. (**b**) Include swings into jumps on floor, on to and from apparatus. (**c**) Roll on mats, including rolling from sitting or crouching on benches or low boxes. (**d**) Take weight on hands after a long arm swing or a short leg swing.

### FINAL FLOOR ACTIVITY                                        2 minutes

Follow your leader's travelling and swinging into a jump.

## NC requirements being emphasised

(a) Exploring different means of swinging, and practising and refining these actions both on the floor and on apparatus.

(b) Making judgements of performances and suggesting ways to improve.

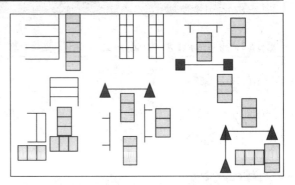

## FLOORWORK

**Legs** (1) Do a preparatory settling and bending in knees and swing of arms to rear before the powerful swing up into jump. (2) The arm swing aims to help the drive given by the ankle joints which should be fully stretched with toes pointing to floor. (3) The 'short run' only needs to be 3 or 4 strides. They experiment with one leg or one arm, or one of each, leading the swing up. (4) Ask observers at a demonstration 'Which part or parts do you think are most helpful in the swinging?'

**Body** (1) While rolling is the activity, 'feeling' the body parts that are swinging your weight, head and shoulders back, then feet forward, is the emphasis. (2) Hands are clasped under knees and head is on to chest to make the body as rounded as possible. (3) A tight curl with no angles sticking out, and a strong sideways swing of the clasped hands and knees, are required to provide the momentum for a complete turn back to back lying.

**Arms** Class will be equally divided in the two ways of swinging up on to hands. Let them find out their favourite, reliable method. The leg kick-up method is easier to control, quicker into position, and better for use on apparatus, later.

## APPARATUS WORK

(1) Standing, two-footed take-offs (across a mat, over a bench) will have a swing from both arms; walking or running take-offs will swing with one leg and/or arm. (2) 'Feel' the leading, swinging parts in going into the rolls. (3) One leg can swing up behind you into a handstand. Two feet and legs can swing up into bunny jumps and handstands. (4) From a standing start, there will be much arm swinging on, and from low apparatus. A good arm swing can also take you to standing or hanging on climbing frames and to hanging on ropes. (5) Plan the sequence under the headings 'pathways' from start on floor to finish on floor; 'rolls', including from being on apparatus; 'weight on hands' after swing of arms or leg. After *planning*, practising and *performing* your sequence, *reflect* on how it might flow more easily and smoothly. Throughout, be aware that the swinging into movement is the most important feature that we are trying to highlight.

## FINAL FLOOR ACTIVITY

One behind the other, try to travel and swing in unison.

## LESSON PLAN • 30–35 MINUTES

### LESSON THEME

Dynamics. (a) Speed. Slow, fast, speeding up or slowing down. (b) Effort. Light, soft, firm, explosive. (c) Whole body tension in stillness, balance, flight and landing. All contribute to better looking, better controlled, more varied and demanding work.

### FLOORWORK                                                    12–15 minutes

**Legs** As you travel in a variety of ways using legs, can you plan to show me a contrast between some small, neat and light actions and some large, strong and lively actions?
**Body** Balance still and stretch a part of your body firmly. From this 'firm' balance, can you relax and move on to another part of your body and balance strongly again? Stretch firmly those body parts that are not being used to support you, and aim for a three or four part sequence.

**Arms** (1) Travelling with arms and legs straight is strong work. Can you show me some examples of slow, strong work? (2) Arms and legs can be firm and straight in cartwheels. (3) They can also be straight while travelling on hands and feet. Can you experiment with the order of moving your four supports? Hands only, feet only; left side, right side; all at same time, bouncing forward with a little lift off floor.

### APPARATUS WORK                                               16–18 minutes

(1) Travel to all parts of the room to visit as many pieces of apparatus as possible. Can you plan ways to cross the apparatus either quickly or very slowly?
(2) Show me a 'firm' balance on apparatus with part or parts of your body stretched strongly. Relax, and move to a new piece of apparatus and demonstrate a new 'firm' balance on different supporting parts.
(3) At your different groups can you plan how to do the following? **Climbing frames** Travel about the frame using arms strongly. **Ropes** Grip the rope so strongly with crossed feet that you can take one hand off at a time and start to climb. Or, swing and practise

taking one hand off and then replacing it, to prove your good foot grip, without which you will never be able to climb. **Trestles** Travel with straight arms and legs above, below and across, and feel how strongly your body is working. **Upturned bench, trestle, box** Balance as a whole group to show me a variety of supporting parts and levels. All relax at the same time as your leader and move on to your next piece of apparatus. **Bench, box** Make a flowing sequence of travelling, rolling and jumping movements. **Mats, bench** Demonstrate slow and fast and/or gentle and explosive movements on apparatus and surrounding floor space.

### FINAL FLOOR ACTIVITY                                         2 minutes

Run, accelerating into an explosive upward leap. Can you land, slowing gently to a stop?

# LESSON NOTES • 4–5 LESSONS DEVELOPMENT

## NC requirements being emphasised

(a) Emphasising changes of speed and effort through gymnastic actions.

(b) Working vigorously to develop strength, suppleness and stamina, and to exercise the heart and lungs strongly.

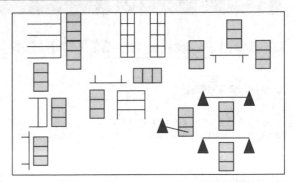

## FLOORWORK

**Legs** The contrasting changes of speed and effort are movement qualities which enhance the appearance of a sequence, and make it look more polished. Easy, quiet, soft, gentle contrasting with strong, vigorous, firm, lively. **Body** If the class are asked to copy the teacher's sagging, limp, lazy balance, then the teacher's firm, strong, fully stretched one with good body tension, they will appreciate and understand which one is hard work to perform, strong, physical and attractive. **Arms** (1) With front, back or side towards the floor, travelling on straight arms and legs is very hard work, even harder as the hands and feet move further apart. (2) Cartwheel travel counts because both feet and hands are main supporters during the action. (3) Hands only can travel forward with straight arms, then stop with body almost straight. Feet can walk forward, alternately, or they can spring forward to land astride feet, depending on the springer's strength and suppleness.

## APPARATUS WORK

(1) A momentary touch on apparatus, as you move quickly on to the next piece, can be with one or both feet or hands, crossing by rolling, vaulting, jumping, twisting, swinging, circling. (2) Once again, only a momentary pause on each piece of apparatus, before moving off to hold a new firm balance, nicely stretched on a different body part. Demonstrate with good ideas for supporting parts, other than the usual ones on feet, or hands and feet. (3) **Climbing frames** Strong hanging, pulling, lowering, circling and rotating, balancing. **Ropes** Pupils can practise the crossed foot action, sole over instep, sitting on the floor, without a rope. The teacher can help by putting hands under someone's crossed feet on the rope. **Trestles** Hanging, swinging, pulling, circling, high crawling. **Upturned bench, trestle, box** A team balance, ideally following leader's timing – on, balance firm, relax, off and away to next one. **Bench, box** Flowing, easy, relaxed, calm sequence, almost non-stop. **Bench, mats** Slow and fast, gentle and explosive are the extremes of contrasting, eye-catching movements. Demonstrate good examples and ask the observers 'Look out for and tell me which pairs of contrasting movements pleased you the most.'

## FINAL FLOOR ACTIVITY

Stillness; slow start into high speed run and dynamic leap; into slow motion landing; to a still finish.

## LESSON PLAN • 30–35 MINUTES

### LESSON THEME

Partner work which provides new experiences not possible on one's own; extends movement understanding because you need to be able to repeat your own movements and be able to recognise your partner's movements; and develops desirable social relationships.

### FLOORWORK                                                  12–15 minutes

**Legs** (1) Follow your leader who is planning to show you three or four different travelling actions. (2) Aim to repeat each action a set number of times, so that you develop to travelling in unison.
**Body** (1) One partner holds a clear, 'firm' body shape which the other copies. Move from held shape to new held shape. (2) Can you plan linking movements which you are both able to perform (rolls; twists; jumps; stretches; etc.)?
**Arms** Show me work on your hands, only, where there is a contrast. For example, one can be long and stretched, one can be tucked up small; one can swing slowly up into position with a long arm movement, one can kick up quickly.

### APPARATUS WORK                                             16–18 minutes

(1) Follow your leader, using only floor and mats to start with. Show your following partner how to cross, go under, along or around the apparatus without touching it. Plan a variety of travelling actions.
(2) New leader, show your partner one touch only on each piece of apparatus, then off to the next piece. Plan a variety of 'one touches'.
(3) At your different apparatus places, can you plan now to do the following? **Climbing frames** Mirror each other's movements on facing frames, and emphasise the pathways you travel along. Are you travelling vertically, horizontally, diagonally, weaving through spaces? **Ropes, bench** Side by side, build up to a matching sequence which can include climbing, swinging, rolling, jumping. **Trestles** Start at opposite ends of the apparatus. Approach, meet, pass and finish in your partner's starting place. **Boxes** One partner travels and stops. The other partner follows and catches up. **Benches** Follow your leader who will show you some work on legs only; then some work on hands and feet only; then some flight and rolls. **Mats** Follow your leader to include a straight pathway on one pair of mats and a zig-zag pathway on the other pair.

### FINAL FLOOR ACTIVITY                                       2 minutes

Facing each other, one mirrors other who leads in a 16 count jump routine which includes 4 sets of simple jumps. For example, feet together, 4; feet apart, 4; feet parting and closing, 4; feet together, turning right round for 4.

# LESSON NOTES • 4–5 LESSONS DEVELOPMENT

## NC requirements being emphasised

(a) Working safely, alone and with others.
(b) Making appropriate decisions and planning their responses.
(c) Practising, adapting, improving and repeating longer and increasingly complex sequences of movement.

## FLOORWORK

**Legs** (1) Follow 2 metres behind partner to be able to see clearly: (a) the actions; (b) exact uses of body parts concerned; (c) body shapes; (d) directions. (2) Building up the sequence, action by action, rather than going into three or four different actions, straight away, will help. This build-up can happen over several weeks if pupils keep the same partners.
**Body** (1) 'A' performs, 'B' copies, after observing: (a) the supporting body parts; (b) the whole body shape; (c) the linking move-

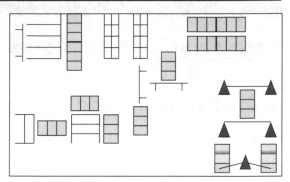

ments, in that order. (2) Leaders have to make allowances for their partner's ability, and include linking movements that they can obviously manage.
**Arms** Ask for simple examples. Bunny jump, landing on same spot; bunny jump that takes you to a new floor space; long, wide cartwheel, travelling; handstand on the spot with bent legs.

## APPARATUS WORK

(1) Follow your leader, 2–3 metres apart, copying leader's actions as he or she negotiates the apparatus, without touching it. Visit all parts of the room, and be aware of others sharing the space. (2) New leader has to 'make decisions quickly', as he or she approaches each new piece of apparatus. What 'quick on and off' actions and uses of body parts are appropriate? (3) **Climbing frames** Remember to show your partner a thumbs under, fingers over grip on the bars for a safe, strong, grip. **Ropes, bench** Side by side with great contrasts of still start and finish, swing through space, smooth roll and a lively jump. **Trestles** Negotiating each other is easier with one stationary and one going under, over or around, at passing place at centre. **Boxes** A series of travels and stops with following partner checking on actions, uses of body parts, body shapes and directions. Keep each part short and uncomplicated. **Benches** If kept simple and using one example only, each time, your partner will be able to shadow you, throughout. **Mats** Jumps and rolls lend themselves to straight and zig-zag pathways.

## FINAL FLOOR ACTIVITY

Pairs will be praised and asked to demonstrate in this activity because they perform exactly in unison, and, more importantly, their ankles full stretching and bending is admirable and quiet.

## LESSON PLAN • 30–35 MINUTES

### LESSON'S MAIN EMPHASES

At the start of the year with a new class we should be aiming to: (a) establish a tradition of listening carefully to the teacher and making an immediate, wholehearted, enthusiastic and vigorous response; (b) create a caring atmosphere of respect for others and self, and always moving carefully and sensibly; (c) establish a well ordered and quiet atmosphere.

### FLOORWORK                                                    12–15 minutes

**Legs** (1) Good running is quiet and you don't follow anyone. Show me your best running and visit every part of the room, the sides, the corners, the ends and the middle. (2) When I call 'Stop!' be in a space all by yourself, well away from apparatus and other children. Stop! (3) As you run, change speed to avoid others and weave in and out of others carefully.

**Body** (1) Stand tall and stretched in your own space. With a three step run, show me a beautifully stretched high jump, with arms stretched to the ceiling. Do a soft 'squashy' landing with knees and ankles bending like springs, gently. (2) Look for a new space near you, and off you go again.

**Arms** Travel about the room on hands and feet, very slowly. When you have lots of space around you, can you spread your body wide as you travel?

### APPARATUS WORK                                              16–18 minutes

(1) Travel to all parts of the room, touching floor and mats only. You can go under, over, along, across and through apparatus, but do not touch any part of it yet.

(2) When I call 'Stop!' show me a clear, firm body shape on the nearest piece of apparatus. Stop!

(3) Next time I call 'Stop!' show me your still, held shape on a different piece of apparatus on a different body part or parts.

(4) Can you show me how you can travel, freely, on all apparatus, using hands and feet as your supports? Where possible, I would like to see you leaving your apparatus with a lively high jump and a soft, quiet, 'squashy' landing.

(5) Now stay at your starting apparatus position to practise, repeat, improve and remember the following. (a) Start and finish away from the apparatus and always be aware of where others in your group are working. (b) Travel up to, on, along, across or around, then away from your set of apparatus. (c) Include travelling on feet, and on hands and feet. (d) Include a beautiful stretch at one or more points. (At start, finish, in flight, in balance.)

### FINAL FLOOR ACTIVITY                                           2 minutes

Lift knees, ankles and arms to make your running quiet and as good as you can make it.

## NC requirements being emphasised

(a) Being physically active.
(b) Responding readily to instructions.
(c) Adopting good posture and the appropriate use of the body.

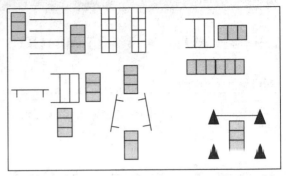

## FLOORWORK

**Legs** (1) Beware of whole class, anti-clockwise running, all following all in a big circle, and common in primary schools. They need to be taught 'Run on straight lines, not curves. Do not follow anyone.' (2) The instruction 'Stop!' given two or three times, makes them run quietly, listening for the signal, and gives practice in 'responding readily to instructions'. Slow responders should be warned to smarten up, and not waste class time. (3) 'Changing speed' includes running on the spot, if necessary, if there is suddenly a crowded area ahead.

**Body** (1) 'Feel your body tension, firming up your arms, trunk and legs in flight. No limp, sagging, lazy body parts, please.'
(2) A two-footed take-off is good for height, and landing with one foot after the other slows down the landing for better control.

**Arms** 'Spreading your body wide' will include long cartwheels, walking on hands with feet apart, travelling on hands and feet, keeping arms and legs long, straight and wide apart, bouncing along on wide hands and feet at the same time, up and down off floor.

## APPARATUS WORK

(1) An exercise in travelling to visit all parts of the room, looking out for space and avoiding impeding others. Occasionally, the teacher should call 'Stop!' to check on the quality of their spacing on the floor, with no queues or overcrowding. (2) 'Stop!' once again is an attention demanding exercise to lay down and demand instant responses. Insist on an immediate response on the nearest apparatus, not some distant favourite. (3) 'Stop!' again, but choose a different apparatus and a different supporting part, which requires good responding and planning. (4) Hands and feet travelling should recall the extensive repertoire from previous years. Teacher commentary gives ideas to the forgetful and acts as a stimulus to all. 'I see and like cat springs along box and benches.' (5) For final sequence, *plan* your pathway up to, on, along and away from the apparatus; your travelling actions on feet, and on hands and feet; and where your beautiful, firm stretch will take place. *Perform*, practise and repeat in a focused way to improve. *Reflect* to inform, adapt, improve and inspire your next *planned* action.

## FINAL FLOOR ACTIVITY

'If I close my eyes, I should not know you are there. It should be so quiet and well controlled.'

## LESSON PLAN • 30–35 MINUTES

### LESSON THEME

Encouraging a tradition of quiet, thoughtful, varied, and continuous work, always with an awareness of good spacing.

### FLOORWORK                                              12–15 minutes

**Legs** (1) Travel from space to space in the hall, using feet only. (2) Plan to include three different actions where one is quiet and easy, one includes a direction change, and one really explodes into a vigorous movement.
**Body** (1) Start with your body crouched low on two feet, knees fully bent, head down to knees. With a strong lunge in one leg, stretch your body fully. (2) Can you stretch your arms strongly upwards in the lunge? (3) Bring the rear foot up beside the forward foot and curl down fully again. (4) Continue your stretching, lunging and curling in different directions with a variety of upper body stretches in the lunge position.
**Arms** (1) Moving slowly, quietly and continuously, can you plan a three part sequence of ways to go from feet to hands and back to feet? (2) Can you aim for variety from different body shapes, or different take-off or landing actions?

### APPARATUS WORK                                         16–18 minutes

In your group places, plan how you can practise, improve and remember the following, where the emphasis is on 'Always be found working, not waiting.' **Climbing frames** As you travel, going through spaces, let different parts lead. **Ropes, mats** In addition to swinging and climbing can you show me two other actions? For example, jumping on to a swinging rope to start with; finishing with a roll on the mat; circling or hanging upside down on two ropes. **Trestles** From a starting position on the floor, well away from teammates, can you all share the apparatus and use all the surfaces? Travelling from a curl to a stretch as we did in the floorwork would be interesting. **Benches** Can you plan to include travelling, rolling and jumping? Travelling can include using hands and feet or feet only on, along or from the benches. Rolls can be from sitting, crouching or kneeling on the benches on to mats. In your explosive jumps you can use benches as springboards. **Boxes** In your continuous circuit, can you cross the cross box with legs straight? Can you include a roll along the return, low, long, box top? **Mats** Balance; roll; balance. You can roll in whichever way you prefer and your roll should be on some body part or parts which are a good starting point for your choice of roll.

### FINAL FLOOR ACTIVITY                                   2 minutes

Run and jump long, and carry on running and jumping without stopping.

## NC requirements being emphasised

(a) Emphasising changes of direction through gymnastic actions.
(b) Making appropriate decisions quickly and planning responses.
(c) Working vigorously to develop suppleness and strength, and to exercise the heart and lungs strongly.

## TEACHING POINTS

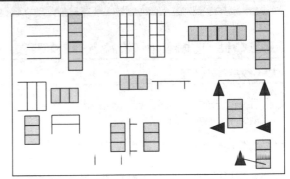

'Be found working, not waiting' is the main emphasis of this lesson and expresses the main feature of good Physical Education, namely that it will be physical.

That it is educational, also, is implicit in the increasing demands now being made for planned, thoughtful and focused performance. For example, in the travelling on feet only, good planning is needed to produce three different actions, with direction changes and a change of effort, one 'quiet and easy, one exploding into vigorous movement.' Such planning and the reflection that follows are continually being emphasised as main NC requirements, second only to the action itself.

Throughout this series of lessons, demonstrate good examples of on-going performances which contain a clear starting and finishing position; quiet, thoughtful, controlled, continuous action; and good responses to the set challenges. Follow-up class reflection and evaluation can now become more specific, enhancing the quality and variety of the work.

In organising the apparatus work the teacher should ensure that he or she is saying 'Please bring out your apparatus, quietly, carefully and sensibly,' in plenty of time to allow the full 16 or 18 minutes for apparatus work which is the most important part of the lesson.

After the three, or at most four sets of apparatus have been visited and worked on, the class are asked to 'Please go back to your own, number one set of apparatus.' Groups bring out and put away the same apparatus because they know where it goes. Apparatus work should be done clockwise and anti-clockwise on alternate lessons, to cover all group places every two lessons.

## LESSON PLAN • 30–35 MINUTES

### LESSON THEME

Development of variety and thoughtful, individual responses which increase the class 'repertoire' of movement.

### FLOORWORK                                                    12–15 minutes

**Legs** (1) Can you link together several ways of travelling where your feet pass each other? (2) Remember that variety can come from different actions, in different directions, at different speeds.
**Body** (1) Choose some part or parts other than your feet to balance on. Stretch firmly those parts not supporting you. (2) Can you change to a new supporting part or parts? (3) Show me your choice of linking movements. Rolls are a very good 'joining up' activity.
**Arms** Pretend the floorboard in front of you is a bench or a low box top. Can you travel along, across or on to this imaginary bench or box, using hands or hands and feet?

### APPARATUS WORK                                              16–18 minutes

(1) As you travel round freely, in and out of apparatus, without touching any, can you remind yourselves and me of the ways you chose to travel where feet pass each other?
(2) When I call 'Stop!' can you show me a still, 'firm' balance on the nearest piece of apparatus? Stop!
(3) When you stop in balance next time, can you show me a balance which copies or contrasts with someone near you? Stop!
(4) At your varied apparatus starting places, repeat, practise, improve and remember the following. **Climbing frames** Start and finish at different places on the floor and travel by changing body shapes. For example, standing and twisting to sit on; curled, stretch up to grip higher; circle round bar to balance, stretched. **Ropes** Practise the main activities that we can do on a rope. We can climb, swing, hang, circle, or a combination of two or more.

**Trestles** Can you vary the body parts that lead you and show me your different travelling actions? (Lying, hanging, sliding, rolling, pulling, twisting can use many combinations of gripping or supporting parts and involve many leading parts.) **Benches** Can you start and finish in a still, balanced position on the floor away from apparatus? In between, can you plan to include flight and rolls and share all the space sensibly with others? **Low boxes, bench** Use your hands strongly to bring you on to, take you along, and help you from the apparatus. Try to include some of the activities you did in the floorwork where we had to pretend that there was a box top or a bench to work on. **Mats** Revise your sequence of balancing movements with the possibility of more adventurous links because of the mats.

### FINAL FLOOR ACTIVITY                                        2 minutes

Follow a leader who will show you his or her ways to travel with the feet passing each other.

58

## NC requirements being emphasised

(a) Exploring different means of balancing and taking weight on hands.

(b) Making judgements of performance and suggesting ways to improve.

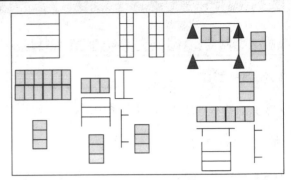

## FLOORWORK

**Legs** (1) Feet 'pass each other' while walking, running, skipping, sliding, galloping. (2) A sequence of three different actions is long enough to be varied and interesting, and short enough to be remembered.

**Body** (1) Teacher commentary and good use of demonstrations will help the class repertoire in this quite difficult activity. Emphasise that 'balance' means that the body should feel like it's wobbling. (2) We do not wobble or sag lazily in the balance, but show firmness particularly in those body parts not supporting us, usually a leg or an arm. On the change to a new balance we relax into the roll, twist, lower, rock, lean linking movement between balances.

**Arms** (1) Pretending that they are working on a bench or a low box top limits the space they need and it gives good ideas for crossing from side to side; on to, along and off; twisting as you travel.

## APPARATUS WORK

(1) As well as feet passing each other, we want pupils to be passing each other, face to face, rather than all following each other, in the big anti-clockwise circle, common in primary schools. (2) Encourage balancing on parts other than feet, or feet and hands which are the most commonly seen. Praise those working hard to give a good body tension from head to toes. (3) The person with whom you choose to contrast might not even be aware that you are contrasting with him or her, as he or she relates to another. 'Contrast' is in the shape, but can be on parts supporting and level used. (4) **Climbing frames** Remind them to keep thumbs gripping under and fingers gripping over bars for a safe, strong grip. **Ropes** Encourage and assist those who are still learning to climb by placing hands under their crossed feet on the rope to give them something to push against. **Trestles** Think about actions and the way that your body parts are supporting you. I might ask for three, quite different examples. **Benches, mats** Flight can come from run along or run up to and jump from cross bench. Rolls can come after landing, and from sitting or crouch on bench. **Low box, bench** A revision of floorwork activity, done 'live'. **Mats** 'More adventurous' headstand or handstand balance, rolling out balance on some other parts.

## FINAL FLOOR ACTIVITY

Ask for emphasis on clear body shape as the way to make it special.

## LESSON PLAN • 30–35 MINUTES

### LESSON THEME

Body parts awareness and how they receive, support balance, lead into and out of movements.

### FLOORWORK                                                    12–15 minutes

**Legs** (1) Can you run and jump high, run and jump long, using good arm and leg actions to help you at take-off, in flight, and on landing? (2) Two-footed take-offs for upward jumps and one-footed take-offs for long jumps are worth trying. (3) Arms can balance you, stretched firmly, forward or sideways.

**Body** (1) Show me three bridge-like shapes, neatly linked. (2) Variety can come from using different supporting body parts – standing; upended on shoulders; or with back, front or side towards the floor. (3) To improve the look and quality of your work, stretch strongly those parts not being used to support you.

**Arms** (1) With your body weight on your hands, can you move your feet in different ways? (2) Can you bunny jump up and down on the spot; cartwheel to a new floor-space; jump feet to a position between hands; jump feet to a position outside hands; hand-walk to a new spot?

### APPARATUS WORK                                               16–18 minutes

(1) Travel freely up to, and on to each piece of apparatus to show a still, stretched, balance on each one.

(2) Still using all the apparatus freely, can you plan to include? (a) Travelling on the floor which is interesting because it uses parts in addition to feet. (b) Actions where the arms take all the weight. (c) A strong upward jump. (d) A still bridge-like position.

(3) **Mats** Revise your sequence of three bridges and improve it by using different supporting parts and different levels. **Climbing frames** As you travel about the whole frame, find body parts on which you can hold a balance. **Ropes** Practise crossed foot grip on your rope. Knees are apart and rope is gripped firmly under sole of one foot and above instep of other. With arms straight, hands together and crossed foot grip, practise a small swing. **Trestles** Plan to find the body parts that can grip the apparatus as you mount on, travel along, around or under, or hold a balance. **Bench, box** Use your legs strongly to bring you on to, take you along, and to help you leave the apparatus. **Benches** Use hands and feet to support you as you zig-zag along the long bench and cross the mat. Use hands to support you as you bring both feet on to cross bench before springing off.

### FINAL FLOOR ACTIVITY                                         2 minutes

Run and jump high; land; lower and roll sideways, curled up small, on to front; take weight on both hands.

# LESSON NOTES • 4–5 LESSONS DEVELOPMENT

## NC requirements being emphasised

(**a**) Exploring different means of jumping, and taking weight on hands, and adapting and refining these actions on the floor and on apparatus.

(**b**) Practising, adapting, improving and repeating longer and increasingly complex sequences of movement.

## FLOORWORK

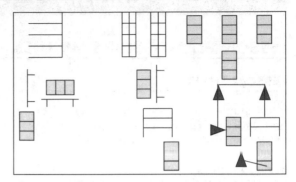

**Legs** (1) Short runs always into your jumps, often back and forward in own space, to avoid impeding others. (2) Be aware of how feet can take off and land, always trying to drive hard and with strong ankles extension, and land with soft 'give' in those ankles. (3) The most obvious firm body tension is seen in the stretched arms which balance you, both in flight and on landings.

**Body** (1) Suggest a trio of bridge-like shapes for those slow to get started, for example: sit (bridge under bent knees); side falling on one hand and one foot; tip toe standing with body arched. (2) Variety also comes from working at different levels, for example: high on tip toes, medium in an arch; low, lying arched. (3) 'Parts not supporting you' are usually an arm or a leg, or one of each. They should be strongly stretched into space.

**Arms** (1) It helps to pretend you are working on or along bench or low box top, as you vault, roll, cartwheel or do twisting bunny jumps. (2) An advanced challenge to see how many of the five tasks they can now achieve.

## APPARATUS WORK

(1) A momentary pause on each piece of apparatus, with a stretched, balance on each, and, ideally, a wide range of supporting parts. (2) A sequence that uses on apparatus and floor all the work practised already on the floor, only. (3) They now stay at one place to practise and improve the following. **Mats** Weight on back of head or shoulders, plus heels, for example, are more comfortable on a mat than on the floor. **Climbing frames** As well as the usual hands and feet, try parts of trunk, behind knees or an elbow. **Ropes** Feel strong enough with hands together and feet crossed, to take one hand away as you swing, and not fall off the rope. **Trestles** Grip with hands in variety of ways; feet in a variety of ways; behind knees; at angle of elbows; under armpits. **Bench, box** An arm swing will help to induce a strong leg action on to and from apparatus. **Benches** Bunny jump, cat spring or cartwheeling actions as you zig-zag. 'Squat jump', i.e. through vault on to cross bench, with hands shoulder width apart and feet placed between hands. Spring off.

## FINAL FLOOR ACTIVITY

The six activities are a good example of a 'longer and increasingly complex sequence of movements.'

## LESSON PLAN • 30–35 MINUTES

### LESSON THEME

Body shape awareness through which to: (a) develop an understanding of and a feeling for body shapes; (b) experience different shapes in held positions, while travelling and in flight; (c) improve the appearance of the work with 'firm' body shapes.

### FLOORWORK                                                        12–15 minutes

**Legs** (1) Can you travel with your leg or legs sometimes stretched? (2) Can you include several actions which satisfy the task?
**Body** (1) Start, lying on front, back or side. Stretch your whole body from finger tips to tips of toes into a long, thin shape. Now change to a curled body where you feel that everything is tucked in, head, arms, legs. (2) Return to your original starting position, stretched out completely or move on to some other supporting parts.

**Arms** (1) Teach cartwheel with its wide, stretched, inverted body. Left hand on floor to side and in line with feet; right hand on floor about half a metre from left and in line with left; jump off both feet and land on right foot beyond right hand in line with hands; push with hands to stretch up, turn body and put left foot in an astride position. (2) Emphasise the left, right, left sequence along a straight line with legs as straight and high as possible. (3) Opposite, of course, if to right is preferred.

### APPARATUS WORK                                                  16–18 minutes

(1) Use all the floor and apparatus, freely, to start with. Show me a clear body shape as you clear the lower apparatus, low boxes, benches and mats, in flight.
(2) Show me a held position on the higher pieces of apparatus, where you have an equally clear body shape.
(3) Can you walk round, practising cartwheel actions on floor, mats and benches? Emphasise the four counts of hand and foot movements and the wide stretch while inverted or partially inverted.
(4) In your starting group places, practise, repeat, improve and remember the following.

**Climbing frames** Start and finish on the floor. Can you twist as you travel, keeping one part fixed to twist against? **Trestles** Using apparatus and surrounding floor, can you show me some bridge-like shapes? **Box, benches** Contrast lively, stretched jumps with easy rolls. **Box, mats** Can you cross the box keeping legs straight? Can you cross the mats keeping arms and legs straight? **Mats** Revise your stretching and curling sequence and introduce more varied levels. **Ropes, bench, mats** Using two ropes, can you circle or hang upside down?

### FINAL FLOOR ACTIVITY                                             2 minutes

Run and jump, stretched; run and jump wide; run and jump tucked, twisted or jacknifed.

## NC requirements being emphasised

(a) Adopting good posture and the appropriate use of the body.
(b) Emphasising changes of shape through gymnastic actions.

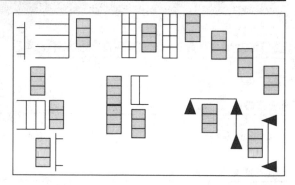

## FLOORWORK

**Legs** (1) Interesting responses include full knees bend to flying stretch; hurdling, leading leg straight, steppings; hopscotch. (2) Contrasting leg actions might include lively running and jumping; soft, giving bouncing with feet together; then hopping with free leg stretched forward.

**Body** (1) This can be a directed activity with the teacher slowly talking the class through it, to ensure a good start for all. (2) Other stretched positions from which to curl can be standing on one or both feet; high upended balance on shoulders; kneeling, arms stretched; headstands and handstands.

**Arms** (1) The 'Hand, hand, foot foot' pattern can be done on an imaginary clock face, placing hands and feet on numbers, e.g. four, two, ten and eight for a simple low angled starter. (2) The straight line target comes with practice and increasing confidence on hands. (3) A handstand practice with legs wide on the spot gives the feeling when in the middle of a cartwheel.

## APPARATUS WORK

(1) Jumping over low apparatus, including across mats, will be from one foot to other or to both after a run, or from two to two after a standing start helped by a swing with one or both arms. (2) Look out for and encourage examples of long stretch, wide stretch, curled, arched, twisted body shapes, supported on an interesting range of body parts. (3) The little walk into cartwheel provides a swing which helps. At the bench, two hands actions on the bench, two feet back on floor. (4) **Climbing frames** Plan the pathway, floor to floor, then plan how to twist part of your body against a fixed part or parts. **Trestles** Back, front or side towards floor and apparatus, and being upended on shoulders, are possible bridges. **Box, bench** 'Contrasts' can include long stretch and tight curl, and explosive jumps and gentle rolls. **Box, mats** Across box, legs can be straight as you roll, high leap, face, gate or astride vault over. **Mats** Handstands, forward rolls; bent leg to straight leg headstands now a possibility on a mat. **Ropes, bench, mats** Hold with hands at shoulder height, so that feet return to floor easily after the circle.

## FINAL FLOOR ACTIVITY

A 3-metre sided triangle will bring you back to your own starting place, and not impede others.

## LESSON PLAN • 30–35 MINUTES

### LESSON THEME

Sequences and children working harder for longer, in almost non-stop action.

### FLOORWORK                                              12–15 minutes

**Legs** (1) Using legs only, can you show me a triangle of movements starting and finishing at the same place on the floor, after three different actions around the triangle? (2) As always, try to start and finish, tall and still. Plan to include varied take-off and landing actions. (3) Different shapes in flight bring great variety to the work.

**Body** (1) Make up a short sequence of favourite balances, in your own floor space. (2) Plan to include different supporting parts for variety and interest and show a 'firm' body in balance each time. (3) Different levels give good variety when you are in your own floor space. Remember – no wobbling!

**Arms** (1) In a handstanding sequence can you plan to include a forward swing on to hands, a sideways swing on to hands, and a few steps on hands? (2) Throughout, keep your arms straight and head forward.

### APPARATUS WORK                                         16–18 minutes

**Climbing frames** Can you plan a travelling sequence which includes: (a) moving hands only, then feet only; (b) moving left hand and left foot, then right hand and right foot; (c) weaving through spaces?

**Ropes** Either try climbing, or show me a group sequence of swinging, going off one after the other and demonstrating variety in body shapes.

**Trestles** In your travelling as you all share the apparatus, use upper and lower surfaces, a variety of supporting parts, and travelling forwards, backwards, sideways, round and across.

**Upturned benches** Use each of the five pieces of apparatus to demonstrate a different balance. Variety will come from varied supporting parts, levels and body shapes.

**Boxes, bench** In your long circuit sequence over boxes and mats one way, and over cross bench the other way, can you: (a) make your hands important in arriving on boxes, and feet important in leaving; (b) do a vigorous spring up off the cross bench to demonstrate a different body shape to the one in front of you?

**Mats** At linked trio of mats, join together two or three agilities (rolls, cartwheels, handstands, etc.). At return, single mat, can you balance, roll, balance across?

### FINAL FLOOR ACTIVITY                                   2 minutes

Can you include examples of stillness, travelling, flight and balance in a short sequence?

## NC requirements being emphasised

(a) Exploring, selecting, developing, refining and repeating a longer series of actions, making increasingly complex sequences of movement.

(b) Sustaining energetic activity and understanding what happens to our bodies during exercise.

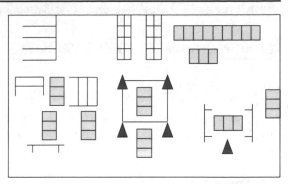

## FLOORWORK

**Legs** (1) A triangle of 3–4-metre sides should not impede others and three actions provide good variety, interest and challenge. (2) Take-offs and landings in jumps, for example, can use one, both or alternate feet. The still start and finish are a good contrast to the vigorous movement. (3) Long stretched, star wide, curled tucked are very 'different'.

**Body** (1) 'Own floor space' means on the spot, no travelling. 'Balanced' means held still, no wobbling. (2) Parts used must be a problem for balancing on, with body having to work hard to be still and under control. (3) High is often on one foot; medium can be an arch, with back, front or side to floor; low, sitting, or on elbow and heel, for example.

**Arms** (1) Forward swing for a still balance. Sideways swing into a cartwheel type action. Handwalking to travel a few steps. (2) Safety from straight arms and head well forward (not looking back under arms) and using just the right amount of force to swing up on to hands.

## APPARATUS WORK

**Climbing frames** Travelling, including alternating hands and feet; alternating sides of body; and weaving through spaces. **Ropes** Group swinging (after a climb), following a leader, but not following another's body shape. 'Variety' should be demonstrated. **Trestles** Group travelling and sharing with much teacher commentary on good actions and good uses of body parts seen. **Upturned benches** One of the group can set the rhythm as they move on to a piece, hold a balance for about 3 seconds, then move on to the next piece. **Boxes, bench** 'Important hands' can vault, roll, twist, lever or bunny jump you on. 'Important feet' can step, jump or bounce you off. **Mats** 'Agilities' mean a strong use of hands somewhere, often with inversion. For example, handstand; lower into a forward roll; stand up and finish with a cartwheel, or dive forward roll; stand and do backward roll with strong arm drive on to feet; cartwheel back to starting place.

## FINAL FLOOR ACTIVITY

The mixture of calm stillness, easy travelling, vigorous leap into flight and the firm balance with non-supporting parts beautifully stretched, all add up to an interesting sequence, pleasing to performer and beholder.

## LESSON PLAN • 30–35 MINUTES

### LESSON THEME

Space awareness and encouraging more adventurous and varied use of own and general space, directions and levels, both to co-operate better with others sharing the space, and to add variety and quality to our movements.

### FLOORWORK                                                    12–15 minutes

**Legs** (1) Can you make up a pattern of movements in your own space with a very small shape on the floor, such as a circle, oval or triangle? (2) Now travel, using the whole floor space and demonstrate the same shape, but on a much bigger scale, back to own place. **Body** (1) Take up a position with one part of your body high. Now move to another balance with all parts close to the floor. (2) Move again and show one part very high. Continue.

**Arms** (1) Cartwheels travel sideways. Handwalking travels forwards. Can you show me ways to travel backwards or diagonally, on hands only, or on hands and feet? (2) On hands and feet, remember that you can have your back or side towards the floor.

### APPARATUS WORK                                               16–18 minutes

(1) Using all apparatus freely, can you travel forwards on to a piece of apparatus and then travel straight along it? Can you travel sideways to the next piece, then sideways along it? Plan ahead to where you are going for such forward or sideways travelling.

(2) Using hands only on the apparatus, can you lift your feet off the floor then push backwards, away from the apparatus, back on to the floor?

(3) In your starting groups of fours or fives at your pieces of apparatus, can you repeat, improve and remember the following? **Climbing frames** Can you zig-zag up, head leading and zig-zag down, feet leading? **Ropes, benches** In your swinging from line to line, bench to line, or line to bench, can you make your legs work at different levels? **Trestles** Can you arrive on and leave the apparatus, using a mixture of front, back or side towards the apparatus? **Boxes, mats** Can you include low level rolls, high level jumps and at least one direction change? **Mats** (1) Can you link two rolls together to show variety? (2) Sideways rolls from kneeling. One leg is stretched sideways. Roll away from the extended leg, tucking chin on to chest. **Benches (one upturned)** Balance walk along upturned bench forward, sideways and backwards. Parts of both feet keep contact with the bench at all times. Zig-zag along return bench and mat.

### FINAL FLOOR ACTIVITY                                         2 minutes

Run and jump into a space and continue without stopping after the jumps.

## NC requirements being emphasised

(a) Emphasising changes of speed through gymnastic actions.

(b) Making appropriate decisions quickly and planning responses.

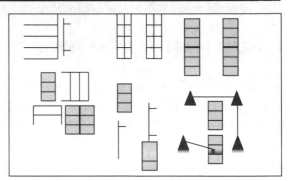

## FLOORWORK

**Legs** (1) 'Pattern' means a repeating series of actions, so there must be at least two activities. Variety from actions, shapes, directions. (2) The second group of repeating actions can be different to the first, but the pathway and shape drawn must be the same.

**Body** (1) High level start position can be on one foot with arm upstretched. Whole body firm and still. A low balance with its element of difficulty can be on seat with arm or leg stretched and/or a leg stretched to a low level. (2) Linking movements become interesting as body weight transfers slowly, and under control. Class can be asked 'When

you watch the demonstration, identify the linking movements that you liked.'

**Arms** (1) Easy on hands and feet. Sideways or diagonally with right arm and leg, then left arm and leg, or bouncing whole body up and from hands and feet moving sideways or backwards. Bunny jumps all ways. (2) Crabbing sideways or diagonally can have back to floor.

## APPARATUS WORK

(1) Demonstrate to extend ways of travelling sideways up to and along the apparatus. For example, slipping sideways on floor, roll sideways on mat; bounce sideways to rope, swing sideways. (2) Instead of the usual passive return of feet to floor, we push strongly to direct feet to where we want them to go. (3) **Climbing frames** Zig-zag on one side up or weaving through spaces. Same down, or sitting weaving bar to lower bar. **Ropes, benches** Legs can hang low, be lifted to horizontal, or can grip rope above head. **Trestles** If the actions on and off are different, like the directions, this becomes an interesting and challenging activity (e.g. walk up trestle

sideways; lie on plank and pull along backwards; or do forward circle over metal pole).

**Boxes, mats** If the low level rolls along mats are slow and smooth and the high jumps are extremely vigorous, these contrasts together with a change of direction, make up a good sequence. **Mats** (1) Forwards, backwards; hands together, hands one in front of other; both hands, no hands; long dive roll, small, curled up roll. (2) A teacher directed activity, helped by one of many pupils who do it well straight away. **Benches** Feel for bench in the balance, then foot down on top. Do not look down. Moving foot runs alongside balance bar.

## FINAL FLOOR ACTIVITY

Run/jump adjusted and variable to let you land in a good space, safely, not impeding others.

## LESSON PLAN • 30–35 MINUTES

### LESSON THEME

Direct teaching of simple, traditional gymnastic skills which are part of our PE heritage – most children enjoy the stimulus of a direct challenge to their skilfulness.

### FLOORWORK                                                    13–16 minutes

**Legs** (1) Skip jumping on the spot, with good stretch of whole body in the air, particularly the ankle joints. (2) Three skip jumps followed by a tuck jump where knees are pulled up as high as possible. (3) Four skip jumps followed by jumping feet astride and together, twice.

**Body** Ski swings. Feet slightly apart. Swing both arms forward/upward above head. Swing arms down past sides, then up above head to high stretch. Long arm swing down and back, with full knee bend; swing arms upward and knees stretch; long arm swing down and back, with full knee bend; swing arms upward and knees stretch; lower arms and repeat.

**Arms** Elbow balance, with hands only on floor. Crouched position with feet apart, place hands under shoulders. Bend elbows slightly to place them inside and under knees. Tilt body forward slowly, from feet on to hands, until toes come off floor, and you are balancing on hands only.

### APPARATUS WORK                                              17–19 minutes

**Mats** (1) Forward roll; stand up with one foot crossed behind the other; twist the body half round to side of rear foot; finish with a backward roll. (2) Lie on back, curled small, hands clasped under knees. Roll to left to right, then try a roll completely over to finish on back again. **Climbing frames** (1) Travel vertically up, diagonally down. (2) With a partner, start at opposite bottom corners. Climb to top corner and come down diagonally, meeting and passing at the centre. **Ropes** (1) Swing with hands gripping together and crossed foot grip. As you swing, can you take one hand off to prove a good foot grip? (2) Rope climbing, using three hand movements to every lift and grip of the feet. One hand up and grip. Other hand up and grip. First hand up and grip next to second hand. Now pull both legs up and grip with crossed feet. 'Hand, hand, hands together, feet up.' **Long box, cross bench** Catspring hands and feet on to near end of long box. Either cartwheel, roll or bunny jump along and from the box. At cross bench, either face vault across on both hands, like bunny jumping, or place hands on bench and astride vault feet on to bench outside hands. Stand up and jump off. **Mats** Bent legs headstand. **Upturned benches** Balance walk forward.

### FINAL FLOOR ACTIVITY                                         2 minutes

Can you plan four groups of four skip jumping activities that are all different?

# LESSON NOTES • 4–5 LESSONS DEVELOPMENT

## NC requirements being emphasised
(a) Developing skill by exploring and making up activities.
(b) Trying hard to consolidate performances.

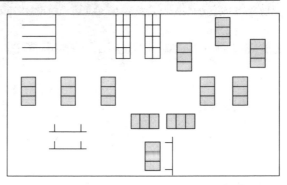

## FLOORWORK

**Legs** (1) Good ankle joint activity, with full strong stretch, is essential for a good, high upwards spring, just as the 'give' in the ankles makes the landing soft and quiet without any jarring. (2) Try to feel your steady rhythm, counting in fours to yourself. A good, fully tucked jump, is a quick, dynamic movement, for which 'trying hard' is necessary. (3) 'Feet together, 3, 4; out and in, 3, 4.'
**Body** The swinging here is a feature of much of our gymnastic activities and is an excellent aid to all kinds of movement, including jumps, handstands, and a one arm swing into a turn as you jump from a box, for example.
**Arms** Rise up on to tip toes and lean your shoulders forward to tilt on to hands. Hands should be pointing forwards with fingers spread.

## APPARATUS WORK

**Mats** Chin on chest forward, heels near to seat to finish with one push only with hands. Hands by ears, thumbs in, going backwards, and strong arm push (thumbs in, still) to land on feet, not knees. **Climbing frames** Keep thumbs gripping under bar, fingers gripping over bar for a safe, strong, reliable grip. **Ropes** The climbing song: 'Hands one, two, hands together, feet up.' Legs pull up with hands together is important. Separate hands mean only upper hand is effective. **Long box, cross bench** Bunny jumps, rolls or cart- wheels represent the degrees of difficulty, in that order. At cross bench, hands on and feet jumped on to bench astride hands is the first stage of the astride vault. **Mats** Bent legs headstand is the easiest 'upended' balance to hold with its triangle base and low centre of gravity. You can go into it from elbow balance. **Upturned benches** Do not look down. Feel for the side of the bar, then feel for the surface where you are to put down your foot, before committing your weight to it. Arms are stretched out to side for balance.

## FINAL FLOOR ACTIVITY

Can you plan four groups of four skip jumping activities that are all different? 'Different' can also include jumps where one foot stays under you and the other reaches out to touch floor at side or front.

## LESSON PLAN • 30–35 MINUTES

### LESSON THEME

Travelling and the many natural body activities and movements which can be experienced, repeated, and improved in a Gymnastic Activities lesson.

### FLOORWORK                                                              12–15 minutes

**Legs** (1) Can you walk, run, jump and land and carry on without stopping? (2) Plan to make your non-stop travelling fit the spaces you are using. Sometimes your walk and run will be very short and sometimes they can spread themselves, when you have room.
**Body** (1) Can you travel by changing from a fully stretched to a tightly curled shape, using different supporting body parts? (2) Your travelling will look more interesting if you change levels. (3) Lunge to crouch on feet; curled to stretched on one side; rolls from stretched, back or front lying; are some of the many possibilities.
**Arms** (1) Can you travel, very slowly, on hands and feet? (2) Cartwheels, handwalks, handstands down with a twist can all be 'travelling', with the emphasis on hands. (3) Strong work on hands and feet usually means straight arms and legs. Hands then feet; one side then the other; bounce up off floor at same time; travelling 'bunny jumps'.

### APPARATUS WORK                                                         16–18 minutes

(1) Using feet only, can you travel, non-stop, to all parts of the room, without touching any apparatus other than floor and mats?
(2) On floor and all apparatus, freely, can you plan ways to travel by changing from a stretched to a curled body shape? Your curled shapes can sometimes take you into a roll to travel to your next stretch.
(3) Stay at your starting group places to practise, improve and remember the following.
**Climbing frames** Partners, one leading, one following. Travel, going from stretches to curls. **Mats** Including a roll somewhere, can you travel along the two mats? **Bench, inverted bench** Use hands and feet to travel along one bench. Show me your different balancing travelling actions along the upturned bench. **Ropes, bench** Practise your good hand and foot grips as you swing from bench back to bench. Climbers, can you do three hand travels to every lift of your feet? One, two, hands together, feet up. **Trestles** Can you travel by bringing hands and feet near to each other, then taking them apart? **Boxes, bench** Can you plan to show me a set of contrasting travelling actions and movements? Smooth rolls; explosive jumps; weight on hands travels; twists, curls and stretches.

### FINAL FLOOR ACTIVITY                                                    2 minutes

Show a partner ways to travel, using legs only, but not including walking, running or jumping.

## NC requirements being emphasised

(a) Practising, adapting, improving and repeating longer and increasingly complex sequences of movement.
(b) Making judgements of performance and suggesting ways to make improvements.

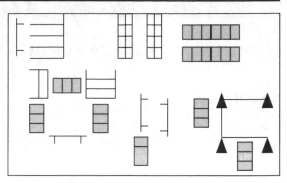

## FLOORWORK

**Legs** (1) Without a still start and finish, the travelling has to continue almost non-stop. This needs quick decision making as they look ahead for space, and adjust to include the three actions set. (2) Landing from the jump will be on one foot to help the change to walking. Often, the landing from the jump is near a wall, corner or busy space, and an instant direction change is needed.

**Body** (1) A short, directed routine of two or three movements, explained by the teacher, helps to get the whole class into action quickly. (2) After the directed start they will gradually, week by week, progress on to adding in their own ideas. (3) In a lunge, legs are spread wide, with front knee well bent, other leg straight to rear. Body leans forward over front leg with arms upstretched above head.

**Arms** (1) Slow travel on hands and feet, rather than quick scampering, means much harder work for the slow, neat actions. (2) Whether cartwheeling or handwalking, straight arms are needed for a safe, strong support, with the head looking forward. (3) Travelling on all fours is a strong activity if arms and legs are wide or close, and straight. 'How high an arch can you make with arms and legs close? How low an arch without collapsing?'

## APPARATUS WORK

(1) Once again, non-stop travelling involves individuals in looking and planning ahead to negotiate apparatus, without touching it, and it involves the whole class in sensible travel, sharing well. (2) Travel by going from stretch to curl, usually by hands and feet closing and parting, is possible on all parts of all apparatus. (3) **Climbing frames** 'A' travels and stops. 'B' catches up. Much hands alone travelling to stretch, then feet curling to catch up. **Mats** Handstand, roll. Cartwheel, roll. Jump and land, roll. Bent leg headstand, tuck head on to chest, roll. **Bench, inverted bench** Balance walk forward, backwards, sideways or cat walk with both hands and feet holding bench. **Ropes, bench** In swinging from bench back to bench, start with a strong upward backward jump to give you, like a pendulum, plenty of swing to bring you back to bench. **Trestles** Hands then feet travel along, under, around, across, again with hands moving alone, then feet moving alone. **Boxes, bench** Non-stop, but with variety in the actions and the effort used.

## FINAL FLOOR ACTIVITY

Hopscotch, bounce, skip, hop, slip sideways, plus many country dance steps, if known.

## LESSON PLAN • 30–35 MINUTES

### LESSON THEME

Dynamics. (a) Time and its varied use in completing actions. Slowly, quickly, slowing down, speeding up, a sudden explosive movement. (b) Flow and the variety of control being applied. From slow, flowing controlled at all times; to flat out vigorous; to linked up, with stops in between each move.

### FLOORWORK                                                          13–16 minutes

**Legs** (1) Show me your best running, weaving in and out of others. Run at slow to medium speeds when near others. Run quickly when you have lots of space. (2) Run and jump and keep on running immediately. Then run, jump and land and be perfectly still; and controlled on landing. Can you feel the difference in these two sets of actions?
**Body** (1) From a standing position, can you sit down and roll back slowly and smoothly on to shoulders and hands? Then, equally smoothly, can you roll back on to your feet? (2) Repeat the whole movement, but plan to add on a quick stretch upwards of legs while on shoulders to end the backward movement, and a quick stretch up of arms to end the forward movement.
**Arms** As you travel about the room, going from feet to hands and back to feet again, can you plan to demonstrate contrasting movements with some vigorous and strong, and some that are flowing and 'easy'?

### APPARATUS WORK                                                    17–19 minutes

(1) Run all round the room, 'easy', steady, speed, touching floor and mats only.
(2) Now run to all parts of the room and show me a vigorous action that brings you on to a piece of apparatus, or takes you across it.
(3) At your different group starting positions can you practise, repeat, improve and remember the following? **Climbing frames** From different starting places on the floor, travel smoothly and continuously before finishing on the floor. **Ropes** (1) Revise swinging with strong crossed foot action, trying to take one hand off to prove a good foot grip. (2) Revise climbing, as in last month's lesson, emphasising three hand moves to every move of legs. **Mats** Revise the rocking and stretching from the floorwork, going from standing to sitting to inverted shoulder balance. **Trestles** As a group, stay on and share all the apparatus and show me a variety of actions. **Box, bench** Accelerate into an explosive high jump from the cross bench. In contrast, show me a slower, more controlled way of travelling along. **Bench, box** Including floor and apparatus, show me a sequence which uses feet to hands and back to feet activities.

### FINAL FLOOR ACTIVITY                                               2 minutes

Can you sometimes run on the spot; at a steady rhythm; accelerate?

## NC requirements being emphasised

(a) Emphasising changes of speed and effort through gymnastic actions.

(b) Exploring different means of rolling, jumping and taking weight on hands, and practising and refining these actions on the floor and on apparatus.

## FLOORWORK

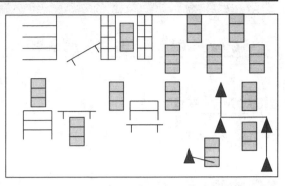

**Legs** (1) 'Weaving in and out of others' means that there will be no following one behind the other, as in the commonplace, anti-clockwise running, all in a big circle, going the same way. (2) Checking the movement alternates with keeping it flowing. A still start, a flowing movement and a checked movement with a still, controlled finish is a way of presenting this pattern.

**Body** (1) Hands swing forward as you lower to balance you, then hands are placed besides shoulders, thumbs in, hands pointing forward, on the shoulder balance. Hands push you forward strongly in swing up. (2) The quick upward stretch of legs while inverted will be an attractive contrast to the slow lowering that preceded it.

**Arms** The kick up to handstand is a strong, vigorous movement and can contrast with the gentle return of feet back to floor. Easy, slow travel on feet and hands can contrast with the dynamic bounce off floor by hands and feet at the same time.

## APPARATUS WORK

(1) 'Feel ... your rhythm; feel ... your rhythm; 1, 2, 3, 4.' Non-stop, easy jogging with heels and hands not as high as in high quality running, feeling your own easy 'cruising' speed. (2) Now there will be acceleration, leading to the mount on to, or the crossing of the apparatus, whether with feet or hands being used to support you as you arrive on, or cross the apparatus. (3) **Climbing frames** This virtually non-stop travelling will need the co-operation of all concerned.

**Ropes** (1) Hands are one on top of other and feet are one on top of other (sole over instep), working as one for a secure grip. (2) Emphasise that hands must be together at the time legs are lifted, the most difficult part.

**Mats** Finish on one leg, or with feet crossed.

**Trestles** Seldom needs an approach from the floor, and a group can stay on for quite long periods, using all surfaces. **Box, bench** The return activity set-up means no queuing and the group can follow, non-stop, as they circulate, demonstrating the contrasts of speed.

**Bench, box** Feet to hands back to feet includes rolls along and from apparatus on to mats; bunny jump actions on to, along and from apparatus; vaults across apparatus.

## FINAL FLOOR ACTIVITY

When space is limited, run on spot. When space is reasonable, run steady. With plenty of room, accelerate.

## LESSON PLAN • 30–35 MINUTES

### LESSON THEME

Partner work to provide new experiences through adapting favourite movement patterns to accommodate another. Pleasurable social relationships are being developed.

### FLOORWORK                                                        16–18 minutes

**Legs** (1) Follow your leader who will show you some lively, warming-up activities, using legs. (2) On the spot, facing each other now, the new leader will demonstrate variations of skip jumping. (eg. feet together; feet apart; feet parting and closing; feet parting and crossing; four, then turn to right, four, then turn to front).

**Body** Partner 'A' holds various bridge-like shapes and 'B' has to wind in, out, through or over, without touching 'A'. Change.
**Arms** First partner performs a movement while weight is on hands or hands and feet. Other partner copies this one movement and adds another. This continues until a 4–6 part sequence has been formed.

### APPARATUS WORK                                                   16–18 minutes

(1) Using all the floor space freely, follow your leader, whose actions are designed to take you around, across, through or astride the apparatus, but touching only the floor and the mats.
(2) New leader, can you hold a bridge-like shape on apparatus, or apparatus and floor, while your partner weaves under, through or over you?
(3) At your starting apparatus places, repeat, practise, improve and remember the following. **Climbing frames** Start at opposite bottom corners. Climb vertically to top corner. Descend diagonally, passing in the centre, to finish in your partner's place. **Ropes, bench, mats** (1) Climb one rope, cross to second rope, descend one after the other (b) Share one rope where leader swings from mat to bench, etc., then passes rope to partner with a swing for him or her to follow. **Bench, inverted bench, trestle, mats** Going from apparatus to apparatus, show your partner a favourite balance. Space permitting, your partner might try to mirror you. **Boxes, mats** Starting at opposite sides, build up to a matching sequence with the emphasis on clear body shapes. **Trestles** Start at opposite ends of the apparatus. Approach, meet, pass and finish in your partner's place. **Mats** One partner lies in various shapes on the mat and other partner has to jump over, showing a matching shape. Change duties.

### FINAL FLOOR ACTIVITY                                              2 minutes

Facing each other, one partner leads in a simple jumping routine on the spot. Groups of four jumps are recommended.

# LESSON NOTES • 4–5 LESSONS DEVELOPMENT

## NC requirements being emphasised
(**a**) Working safely, alone and with others.
(**b**) Making appropriate decisions quickly and planning their responses.
(**c**) Making judgements of performance and suggesting ways to improve.

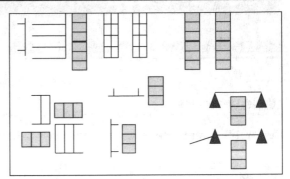

## FLOORWORK

**Legs** (**1**) 'Lively' infers vigorous, powerful, wholehearted, strong. (**2**) Establish a joint rhythm which can almost be felt and heard, so that your duo could almost keep going with eyes shut. It is a fairly slow rhythm if there is a dynamic drive from strong ankles giving a high lift.

**Body** Still partner can make three bridges, one after the other, to give travelling partner some variety, from an easy high bridge on both feet with body angled forward, down to a difficult low level arch, say, on elbows and knees.

**Arms** This gradual build-up activity is most popular with all pupils. Partners need to make considerate allowance for each other only showing something within other partner's capability. The build-up extends over the four or five week period of this lesson, and they don't need to do all in one lesson.

## APPARATUS WORK

(**1**) Practise following at 2 metres behind leader to see easily the actions, uses of body parts, shapes and directions being offered. (**2**) The weaving of the floorwork transfers to apparatus, or apparatus and floor, as they circulate to each apparatus in turn. A high arch with back or front towards apparatus is a quick method. (**3**) **Climbing frames** Starting on opposite sides will let you mirror each other with hands, feet and bodies moving in unison. **Ropes, bench** Climb half way, then carefully cross to next rope. In the swings, remember to jump up and back at start of swing to produce a big pendulum action for a long enough swing. **Benches, trestle** Contrasting supporting parts and shapes would be a good challenge as they circulate, balancing alternately. **Boxes, mats** Agree the actions, then decide on body shapes to be emphasised and any direction changes. Will there be a spectacular change of speed or effort at some point? **Trestles** Passing on a plank is easy with one sitting or crouching, one going over. Passing on a metal pole is very difficult, with one above and one below. **Mats** Matching tucked, wide star, long stretched, arched or twisted shapes.

## FINAL FLOOR ACTIVITY

Simple foot movements (together, parting and closing, turning to face each wall) can be enhanced by the addition of matching arm movements (swinging to side, front or above head).

## LESSON PLAN • 30–35 MINUTES

### LESSON THEME

Re-establishing those essential traditions without which the optimum levels of enjoyment, safety and achievement will never be realised: **(a)** all reacting immediately to the teacher's instructions; **(b)** all unselfishly sharing floor and apparatus space to promote safety and good working conditions; **(c)** all contributing to a co-operative, quiet, working atmosphere.

### FLOORWORK                                                12–15 minutes

**Legs** (1) Can you change quietly and smoothly between running and other activities such as walking, running and skipping? (2) Can you change, also, between actions on the spot, when your floor is crowded, and movements when you travel more widely when space permits? Keep looking as you move.

**Body** (1) Can you travel, going from a wide body shape to a new wide shape? (2) You can be standing; lying; on hands and feet; with one side to floor on one hand and foot.
**Arms** (1) Which parts of your body can give you a swing up on to hands? (2) Try long arms starting above head; one foot kicking up behind you; one arm leading into a cartwheel; two arms and one leg.

### APPARATUS WORK                                           16–18 minutes

(1) Walk quietly all round the room, touching floor and mats, and keeping well away from all others.
(2) Change to your best running, carefully weaving in and out of apparatus and others. When I call 'Stop!' show me a wide shape on the nearest piece of apparatus. Stop!
(3) Stay at your number one apparatus to practise, improve and remember the following. **Climbing frames** Make short travels into a balance, particularly trying to show a 'firm', wide body shape. **Ropes, mats** Revise rope climbing, saying to yourself 'Hand, hand, hands together, feet up', aiming for a stretched body afer the three hand movements. **Trestles** Find as many parts of the trestles, or trestles and floor, as possible, to balance on. **Benches, mats** (1) Can you make your hands important in travelling along or across the benches? (2) Show me ways to go from benches on to mats. **Cross bench, mats** Drive up and off the cross bench using one or both feet. At return mats, can you show me a balance, roll, balance sequence? **Boxes, mats** Face vault, i.e. 'bunny jump', over the low, cross boxes.

### FINAL FLOOR ACTIVITY                                      2 minutes

Travel on legs and swing up into a turn to a still landing, using arms well for balance.

# LESSON NOTES • 4–5 LESSONS DEVELOPMENT

## NC requirements being emphasised

(a) Exploring different means of taking weight on hands.
(b) Being physically active.
(c) Responding to instructions.

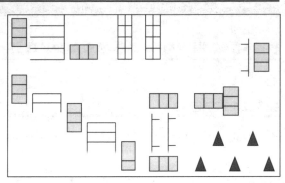

## FLOORWORK

**Legs** (1) Running has to link pairs of other activities. One of the activities can be slow as you look for a space, for your run into the third activity which can be more lively. (2) Pupils seldom practise working on the spot, when there is a sudden crowding. Every leg activity can be performed in your own space which provides an attractive contrast to the free movement.

**Body** (1) From wide to wide shape is unusual and quite difficult. A directed start by the teacher will help to get everyone moving. From the directed start, week by week, they can add and develop their own ideas for supporting parts and linking movements. (2) The standing high level; medium level, arched on hands and feet; and the low level side falling with one side towards floor, on one hand and one foot, provide a good example of varied levels.

**Arms** (1) They will have gone up on to hands hundreds of times, possibly without thinking about where the impetus is coming from. (2) Long arms swing from above head is a slow, powerful, long lever action used by most pupils to start with. The one foot swing/ kick up behind body gives a quick, neat, more easily controlled swing.

## APPARATUS WORK

(1) The floor circulation, without touching any apparatus, is an exercise in sharing the floor, keeping well away from others, not all following one another round or queuing. (2) 'Stop!' is an exercise in 'reacting immediately to instructions', setting a standard of responsiveness for the year. (3) **Climbing frames** Balances look better and are harder physically when we stretch out fully the parts not supporting us. **Ropes** Revise, if necessary, the strong, crossed feet grip position, with sole over instep, that grips you when you take one hand off to climb up. **Trestles** One foot and hand; two hands; two feet; lying on tummy, plus many balances using floor and part of trestle. **Benches, mats** Pull along on back or front; bunny jump or cartwheel across; feet off and on alternately as hands support along; jump feet between or astride to standing on, jump off. **Cross bench, mats** The vigorous run and spring off bench can contrast with the more restrained balance, roll, balance. **Boxes, mats** Hands on box; bunny jump up with high hips; twist round to land, facing box all the time in the face vault.

## FINAL FLOOR ACTIVITY

A short 3–4 metres travel into a swing up into a turn can be done back and forward in own, small corridor.

## LESSON PLAN • 30–35 MINUTES

### LESSON THEME

Re-establishing the tradition or quiet, varied, thoughtful, continuous work. Good spacing to prevent frustration and allow safe practice is also being strongly emphasised.

### FLOORWORK                                              12–15 minutes

**Legs** (1) Can you run and jump high, run and jump long, using good arm and leg positions to help you balance in flight and on landing? (2) What take-off actions of feet help long and high jumps? (3) What arm positions best help you to balance on landing?
**Body** (1) Practise and link together any big body movements while standing, upended on shoulders, or with your front, back or side to the floor. (2) Body movements include curling, arching, stretching, twisting.
**Arms** Still thinking of natural body movements, can you travel, slowly, with your weight on your hands, or hands and feet, by changing body shape?

### APPARATUS WORK                                          16–18 minutes

**Climbing frames** Climb vertically. Try to twist down, legs leading, using hands and arms only for support. Use crossed hands grip, sitting on top bar, one hand gripping towards you, the other gripping with knuckles away from you. Lower body by rotating to near hand side.
**Ropes** Use two ropes to show a sequence that includes curling, circling and hanging upside down. **Upturned benches** Cat walk along upturned bench on all fours with weight evenly distributed between hands and feet, with knees and hips low. As a contrast, balance with body tall and stretched. While waiting your turn on the benches try some other balancing on the mats (e.g. elbow balance or bent leg headstand). **Boxes, mat** Can you cross the cross box using hands only? Can you return along the long box, using legs only? **Mats** Revise and expand your floorwork sequence of linked large body movements. Working on the mats means that you can be a bit more adventurous (e.g. rolls can be more comfortably used as ways to link movements together).

### FINAL FLOOR ACTIVITY                                      2 minutes

Can you plan and show me a triangle of three jumps back to your starting position? Make one high, one long and one of your choice (e.g. tucked, jacknife, star).

## NC requirements being emphasised

(a) Exploring, developing, practising, refining and repeating a longer series of actions, making increasingly complex sequences on floor and using apparatus.

(b) Working vigorously to develop suppleness and strength, and to exercise the heart and lungs strongly.

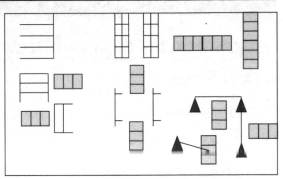

## FLOORWORK

**Legs** (1) Plan start and finish positions on floor. Plan to do runs and jumps, there and back to starting place, or to move round room. (2) Long jump is helped by one-footed take-off. High jump is helped by two-footed take-off. You can land with feet together or apart, or with one foot arriving after the other, slowing you down. (3) Stretched arms give good shape and help balance, usually stretched to front or to sides.

**Body** (1) Pretend you are in a large bubble and try to push its sides away from you, stretched or wide. (2) 'Big' means involving whole of body which includes big outwards as in stretching, or a big curl, tightly inwards.

**Arms** Ask for slow, careful whole body movements, not quick little scampering where body weight is mostly on feet anyway. Long crawls until body is almost horizontal; bunny jumps with shoulders over hips over hands; cat springs (flight from feet on to hands); bouncing with whole body coming up off floor; crab; cartwheels.

## APPARATUS WORK

**Climbing frames** Thumbs are curled under bars for a safe, strong grip. The 'rotary travelling' descent is a strong arms and abdominals action. **Ropes** When circling or hanging upside down, it is important to grip rope at shoulder height with bent arms to ensure feet return safely to standing on floor. **Upturned benches** In cat walk, centre of gravity must be kept low with knees well down below level of bench. Hand, hand, foot, foot travel with a strong hand grip. Feet are balanced on top of bench. **Boxes, mats** In crossing box with hands only, experiment by approaching box from front, at an angle, and even side towards. One or both hands can support you, and you can cross with back towards the box. **Mats** A moving 'bubble' of large body movements, now on mats, can include handstands, cartwheels, crab arches and dive rolls.

## FINAL FLOOR ACTIVITY

The interesting variety provided by the different shapes can be expanded by varied take-offs and landing actions in the jumps. Take-off can be from one or both feet. Landings can be on to both feet together or apart, or on to one foot, then the other for a slower, controlled finish.

## LESSON PLAN • 30–35 MINUTES

### LESSON THEME

Jumping and landing, rolling and balancing.

### FLOORWORK                                           12–15 minutes

**Legs** (1) Show me a beautifully stretched and balanced starting position on tip toes or on one foot. Run a few steps and swing up into a high jump with a turn in flight or on landing. Finish, beautifully stretched and balanced. (2) How are you holding your arms to help balance in flight and on landing? (3) A landing with feet astride, or one foot landing after the other, slowly, also helps to control your finish.

**Body** (1) Log roll. With feet tight together, body fully stretched and arms stretched upwards, show me a sideways roll with your straight body. (2) Circle roll. Start, sitting in the straddle position, with feet wide apart. Move sideways, keeping legs wide apart and straight as you lower on to back. Keep your piked hips, hold your shape as you continue to roll sideways on your back. Finish, having made a half-turn, to face the opposite way.

**Arms** (1) Put both hands on the floor under your shoulders. Do three little preparatory bounces of feet off floor, keeping arms straight and head looking forward. On the fourth big bounce go up into your bunny jump with knees kept well bent. (2) Remembering that bent leg position, try a handstand where you let bent legs 'dangle' down over head, helping balance.

### APPARATUS WORK                                      16–18 minutes

(1) Use all the floor and apparatus freely to show me: (a) a still, ready position on tip toes; (b) a short run and jump into a turn on landing in balance; (c) a roll on mats or floor; (d) a balance on any piece or pieces of apparatus. (2) At your starting apparatus position, practise, improve and remember the following.

**Climbing frames** Show me a balance: using floor and frame; with body through one of the spaces; and on one outside of the frame.

**Ropes** Climb after a strong upward jump to place both hands high and together, or run and jump into a strong swing which ends in a well balanced landing. **Trestles** Can you show me parts of the apparatus where you can hold a 'firm' stretched balance on three body parts, then two body parts, then one body part? **Inverted benches, trestle** Bent leg headstand on the mats. Hands and forehead placed on mat to make a triangle. With weight equally on forehead and hands, feet walk in to raise hips above point of support. Knees bend to raise feet from floor. **Boxes, bench** Plan to include jumping, rolling and balancing. **Mats** Revise your floorwork rolls and show me how you can link two or more rolls together.

### FINAL FLOOR ACTIVITY                                 2 minutes

Balance; run and jump; balance.

## NC requirements being emphasised

(**a**) Exploring different means of rolling, jumping and balancing and adapting and refining these actions on the floor and on apparatus.

(**b**) Making appropriate decisions quickly and planning responses.

(**c**) Making judgements of performances and suggesting ways to improve.

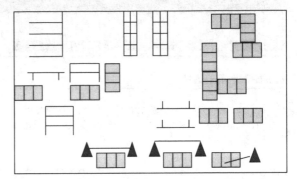

## TEACHING POINTS

### Anticipation, realisation and retrospect

If a good Physical Education lesson is 'like a good meal because you look forward to it, enjoy it, and remember it with great pleasure, and it has well-planned, satisfying variety', then this lesson should appeal. It has varied and lively, vigorous, exuberant running and jumping, contrasting with the more flowing, controlled rolling, contrasting with the still, firm balances.

### Planning, performing and reflecting

Emphasise to the pupils the importance of planning before performance so that, for example in the apparatus sequence, they could tell you:

(**a**) their starting and finishing positions on floor and in body

(**b**) the place where they run and jump into a turn on landing

(**c**) which body part and piece of apparatus will be used for balance

(**d**) where they will do their roll.

Emphasise, also, the value of reflecting immediately after their performance and trying to work out how to improve it next time. Often this reflecting and evaluating is inspired by the teacher, commenting in passing, or as a result of a demonstration given to the rest of the class and their follow-up comments, or as a result of seeing someone else's demonstration bringing out an interesting feature.

In NC terms, the pupils need to be 'put in the picture; regarding the importance attaching to thoughtful planning and preparation as the basis for performance; to focused participating in the thoughtful way that enables reflection; and to reflecting and evaluating to bring in any changes or adaptations, as necessary, in their subsequent performances.

## LESSON PLAN • 30–35 MINUTES

### LESSON THEME

Body parts awareness and thinking beyond the action to how the hands, feet and larger body surfaces are working to carry, support, propel, grip and act generally.

### FLOORWORK                                                    12–15 minutes

**Legs** (1) Take three walking steps, then do a hop. Step on to your non-hopping foot first. (2) Take three walking steps then do a long step. As before, start with the non take-off foot. (3) Now jump from one foot to both feet. (4) Can you join a hop, a step and a jump, starting with three walking steps?

**Body** (1) Hold a still, starting position on a part or parts of your body. Show me different ways of moving your body on to a new supporting part or parts. (2) The sequence will be improved if you change levels. (3) Rolling, rocking, twisting, lowering, levering, jumping, swinging are among the many we have used.

**Arms** (1) Elbow balance. From a crouched position with feet apart, place hands on floor and under shoulders. Bend elbows slightly to place them inside and under knees. Tilt body forward slowly, from feet on to hands, until toes come of the floor. (2) Show me a favourite way of taking weight on hands.

### APPARATUS WORK                                               16–18 minutes

(1) Using feet only, show actions you can use to take you along, over, across, around, through apparatus, without touching any.

(2) Using hands only, show me one touch only on apparatus where your touch can take you across, along or simply up into a balance.

(3) At your apparatus starting places, can you practise, improve and remember the following? **Climbing frames** From a fixed position on one body part, can you travel by twisting, lowering, circling, pulling, levering strongly on to some other part? **Ropes** As you take off, swing and land, can you include varied actions at take-off and on landing? **Trestles** Use your arms strongly to bring you on to the apparatus. Plan ways to use them to grip, pull, support as you travel. And finally, can you make your hands important as you leave the apparatus? **Bench, box** Squat jump on to cross bench. Hands are shoulder width apart on the bench and feet are jumped on to bench, between hands. Jump off with a stretched or star jump. Squat jump on to end of long low box then use hands to help you along and from the box. **Mats** Revise your floorwork transferring from body part to body part. Emphasise how you do the transfer. **Box, bench** Plan a sequence that includes vigorous jumps with soft landings, rolls and a slow body movement somewhere to contrast with the lively jumps.

### FINAL FLOOR ACTIVITY                                         2 minutes

Sit with legs straight. Turn to front support. Jump feet to crouch. Spring up. Cartwheel.

## NC requirements being emphasised

(a) Developing skill by exploring and making up activities.

(b) Trying hard to consolidate their performances.

## 'What exactly is happening within our movements?'

is what we are concentrating on in this lesson.

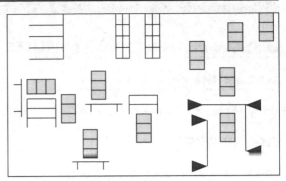

This focus on our body parts and studying their exact actions takes us into the area of good quality and correct and safe techniques. 'Let your knees "give" on landing from a high jump'; 'Tuck your chin on to your chest (to safeguard head) as you roll forward'; 'Keep your arms straight in your handstand'; 'Thumbs under the bar, fingers over, in climbing'; 'Thumbs forward when doing a downward circle on a bar or pole'; 'Hands together when pulling up on a rope climb', etc.

When we train pupils to be good observers of movement to help them to make comments, judgements and even suggestions for improvement, we emphasise that the first two features they look out for are the actions being performed and the exact uses being made of the body parts involved.

Body parts awareness leads to better body management and self-control. Such awareness comes from focusing on self and own movement. A greater repertoire and awareness of the huge range of body part uses is also developed by observing demonstrations and by the direct teaching of jumping and landing, climbing, rocking, rolling, lowering, tilting, twisting, springing, levering, overbalancing and leaning as methods of receiving, transferring and propelling our body weight.

Body parts awareness helps to improve control of our body shape, enhancing the appearance of the work, and making greater physical demands to make the whole body firm.

Variety and contrast are two desirable features in a good Gymnastic Activities performance. Both are enhanced by an awareness of the many actions possible and the many ways in which body parts can function, in response to a challenge from the teacher. For example, stepping is only one of many 'travelling on feet' actions, but an awareness of the different actions and uses of body parts possible within stepping can produce great variety and contrast – on tip toes, heels, inside and outside of foot; with straight, slightly bent, very bent knees; swinging leading leg forward, to side, across you, behind before putting it down in front; in forward, sideways or backward directions.

## LESSON PLAN • 30–35 MINUTES

### LESSON THEME

Body shape awareness and a constant concern for good looking, poised movements.

### FLOORWORK 12–15 minutes

**Legs** (1) Walk smartly and briskly round the room as if you are on an important errand. Erect body with arms and legs swinging forward well stretched. (2) Change to your best running where there is a look of 'lifting' in heels, arms, head and chest. (3) Now show me some running, jumping and landing where there is a clear body shape at all times. **Body** Stand, stretched on tip toes; lower into a bridge on hands and feet; lower back on to seat and roll up to a stretched shoulder balance; twist bent legs over one shoulder to curled kneeling. Stand and repeat, and feel the many different body shapes you are holding or passing through.

**Arms** (1) In your handstanding or handwalking, experiment with legs stretched or bent, feet together or apart. (2) Balance is helped by very bent legs 'dangling' down low over head and by leg making a straight line, one forward, one held back, like a tight rope walker's pole.

### APPARATUS WORK 16–18 minutes

(1) Run freely all round the room, touching floor and mats only. When I call 'Stop!' show me a clear body shape on the nearest piece of apparatus. Stop!
(2) Next time I stop you, can you match or contrast your body shape with that of someone near you. Stop!
(3) **Climbing frames** Can you travel to all parts of the frame, including going through spaces, by changing from a stretched to a curled body? **Ropes, mats, bench** (1) Revise your climbing, emphasising the 'one, two, hands together' to take hands up to a full stretch, followed by the full lift of both legs to their next gripping position. (2) Swing and land on the mats with your body small and curled, then swing and land on the bench with your body almost straight. **Trestles** Can you use all the apparatus to show me held body shapes and shapes that you travel through? **Benches, mats** Run and jump high off the cross bench to show a different shape to the one who went before you. At the return long bench and mat, show me travelling actions where the body is straight, curled or wide. **Boxes, mats** Travel along the long box, demonstrating long body shapes. Travel across the cross, wide box, including at some point a wide body shape. **Mats** With a leader setting your group rhythm, practise again your floorwork sequence. Stretched on tip toes; bridge on hands and feet roll to shoulder balance; twist to kneeling.

### FINAL FLOOR ACTIVITY 2 minutes

Choose four neat body shapes, two on your left, and two on your right foot. Can you travel through each in turn on to the next?

## NC requirements being emphasised

(a) Emphasising changes of shape through physical actions.

(b) Adopting good posture and the appropriate use of the body.

## FLOORWORK

**Legs** (1) Start by praising those who are standing well, head up, shoulders back, arms by sides, and weight slightly forward on balls of feet, in a 'ready to go' position, and still, without fidgeting. (2) A quiet, lifting action works up from heels, through knees, arms, chest and head, all on the balls of the feet. Feeling is of 'up'.

**Body** This directed sequence of four, varied, still, bridge-like shapes is led by the teacher and is a quick way to produce whole class activity. It shows a variety of supporting parts and body shapes. Pupils will move on to developing their own variations.

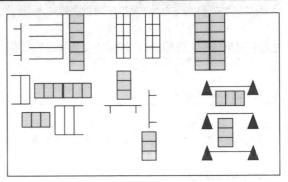

**Arms** (1) Because arms will always be stretched when inverted to ensure a safe, strong support for the whole body, variations of body shape will come from the leg positions, including, for example, one leg bent and one leg straight.

(2) 'Dangling legs' lower the centre of gravity to help balance.

## APPARATUS WORK

(1) A quick reaction and instant planning are needed to stop, go to nearest apparatus, and demonstrate a clear body shape. The teacher encourages balance on parts other than feet or feet and hands. (2) Pairs of adjacent performers now have to react quickly to present matching or (more difficult) contrasting body shapes. This activity deserves to be demonstrated, giving pleasure to several pairs and helpful ideas to everyone observing. (3) **Climbing frames** There will be much feet only, then hands only travelling. **Ropes, mats, bench** (1) Hands together do the pulling, not the hand well above hand, often seen, where the bottom hand only works. (2)

Inspire a full swing by a strong up and back jump to give you a long, pendulum like swing long enough to deliver you. **Trestles** A good challenge is 'Can you alternate still, held shapes with travelling shapes?' **Benches, mats** At cross bench, let one in front of you go, see the shape, then follow. At long bench, straight pulls, curled tight bunny jumps, wide, low cartwheels over, side to side. **Boxes, mats** Along with cartwheels, dive rolls, upward spring from crouch, pulls. Across with star jump off, low cartwheel across, hands on and feet wide astride on. **Mats** Group can be on opposite sides of mat, facing a space, with leader central.

## FINAL FLOOR ACTIVITY

Go from left to right to left to right.

## LESSON PLAN • 30–35 MINUTES

### LESSON THEME

Partner work to: (a) explore ways to work with another to create movements not possible when working alone; (b) gain a better understanding of own and others' talents and limitations.

### FLOORWORK                                                    16–18 minutes

**Legs** (1) Follow your leader who varies the travelling by way of: (a) using different parts of the foot; (b) varied directions; (c) varied shapes, tall, wide, small curled. (2) Other leader takes over and leads, varying the work by: (a) changing speeds; (b) adding on unusual arm or leg 'gestures'.
**Body** Take up a position near each other.

Can you find different ways to grip each other and lean away from each other into a combined balance?
**Arms** Partner 'A' takes up a strong position on hands and feet at a low level. Partner 'B' has to cross 'A' by taking weight on hands. ('A' has to make enough low, wide gaps to assist this.)

### APPARATUS WORK                                              16–18 minutes

(1) Follow your leader, using floor and mats only, walking, running and jumping when the available space makes these actions safe to use and appropriate.
(2) One partner balancing, one partner giving a little support, hold a balance on a piece of apparatus, where the balance is perfectly firm, stretched and still. Change duties, still only giving minimum help to balance.
(3) **Climbing frames** Start, side by side, at floor level. Can you travel upwards, sideways and down diagonally, together, showing good body shapes? Can you be aware of the shapes you are making as a pair? **Ropes** Rope each, starting facing each other. Can you make up a matching sequence which includes three examples of variety, such as body shapes used in travelling; directions used in travelling or

on landing; methods of starting a swing. **Trestles** Start exactly opposite each other. Mirror each other's movements. Can you include a variety of travelling actions? **Bench, upturned bench** Follow your leader across bench on to mats where leader completes the first movement and waits for partner to copy and follow. On the return upturned bench can you both balance along, and keep some form of body contact? **Boxes, mats** Start at opposite ends of apparatus. Can you approach, meet, pass and finish in partner's starting place? On either box, can one partner hold a bridge for the other to negotiate? **Mats** Show your partner a favourite sequence of linked agilities. Your partner will observe carefully, then make one helpful suggestion for an improvement.

### FINAL FLOOR ACTIVITY                                         2 minutes

With partner's support, show me a balance you could not do on your own. Each has a turn.

## NC requirements being emphasised

(a) Working safely, alone and with others.
(b) Practising, adapting, improving and repeating longer and increasingly complex sequences of movement.

## FLOORWORK

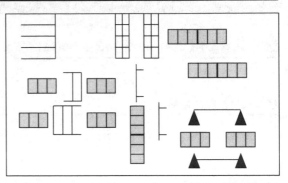

**Legs** (1) Follow 2–3 metres behind to be able to see actions, body parts activity, shapes and directions easily. A routine of three activities is enough for one to plan and one to copy. (2) Second leader keeps same actions but expands them with a change of speed at one point, and a gesture, pointing with a body part.

**Body** Lean away in identical or different standing, kneeling, sitting, side falling (on one hand and foot, side to floor), horizontal balance standing on one leg with trunk horizontal, crab, etc.

**Arms** Partner crossing is looking for low arms, legs, back, best helped by long, low, wide star shape held by 'strong position' partner whose front, back or side can be towards the floor.

## APPARATUS WORK

(1) If the three actions are simple the pair can do them in unison, always looking for spaces and sometimes performing on the spot, one behind the other, when floor is suddenly crowded. (2) Minimum support, occasionally removing support for a moment as partner struggles to 'Hold it!' (3) **Climbing frames** Travel up, then along to opposite side, and then diagonally back to start. A particular shape or shapes could be emphasised during each third. **Ropes** Plan: three or four actions; then uses of body parts concerned; then shapes; then changes of direction or levels.

**Trestles** From matching start on signal of one of pair, approach, mount apparatus, leave apparatus, and travel to partner's starting place. Build up to performing in unison by keeping actions simple. **Bench, upturned bench** Contact along inverted bench by walking, one forward, one back; both sideways; both forwards; one holds other who sits down on bench, etc. **Boxes, mats** At point of passing, one can be stationary, low to go over, high to go over. **Mats** 'Agilities' mean activities mainly upended, supported by hands.

## FINAL FLOOR ACTIVITY

For example, horizontal balance standing on one foot, with upper body leaning forward as near horizontal as possible, and with both arms upstretched above head. Partner helps by placing a hand under one of partner's hands.

## LESSON PLAN • 30–35 MINUTES

### LESSON THEME

Space awareness with an emphasis on making good and varied use of the floor and air space around us and the apparatus.

### FLOORWORK                                                    12–15 minutes

**Legs** (1) One half of the class run and jump, pushing arms and legs out strongly to take up as much air space as possible. The other half do quiet little jumps on the spot, taking as little air space as possible. The running and jumping, lively group must look for, then run into a new space each time. (2) Change over duties.

**Body** (1) Balance on your shoulders and explore your surrounding 'bubble' of space with your feet. (2) Lower to kneeling and explore your space 'bubble' with hands and upper body. (3) Are there any other starting positions from which you can reach out far into all parts of your space 'bubble'?

**Arms** Place both hands firmly on the floor. Move in as many ways and to as many places as you can without moving hands.

### APPARATUS WORK                                              16–18 minutes

**Climbing frames, bench** Start at the bottom corner or bottom of bench. Zig-zag your way to the top corner of the frame, and then come down diagonally to the opposite corner.

**Rope, mats** (1) Can you climb from rope to rope, getting higher each time? (2) Can you swing from mat to mat, or floor to mat, with legs at different levels? Can you include a direction change in the air or on landing?

**Trestles, planks, pole, mats** (1) Travel, using all apparatus, with your body near to the apparatus. (2) Travel, using all apparatus, with many parts of your body high above or stretched, well away from the apparatus.

**Bench, upturned bench, trestle, mats** (1) Try some easy balances where you are low over your supporting parts. (2) Try some balances where you are tall, wide, stretched and well above your supporting parts. Tall is harder to hold but better looking and more satisfying.

**Boxes, mats** As you travel up to, on, along and from the apparatus, use as much air space as possible.

**Mats** Link two rolls together where one is small, curled tight and not needing much space, and the other is bigger and needing more space.

### FINAL FLOOR ACTIVITY                                        2 minutes

Practise an 'easy' jump in your own space, making a simple pattern or shape on the floor. Then travel about the whole space, repeating a big version of your pattern, and using much livelier actions.

# LESSON NOTES • 4–5 LESSONS DEVELOPMENT

## NC requirements being emphasised

(a) Emphasising changes of direction, level and use of own and shared space, through gymnastic actions.

(b) Exploring different means of jumping, balancing and taking weight on hands.

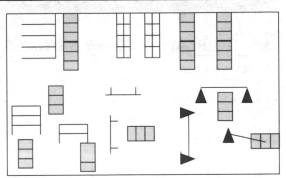

## FLOORWORK

**Legs** (1) Often the air space, above, to front, rear and side of us, is not sufficiently considered in Gymnastic Activities. Here, it is the main consideration. (2) Often, we omit to perform on the spot, as we should do, when the floor ahead is suddenly crowded. Here, it is our main thought.

**Body** (1) Feet will split and reach to front, rear and to sides. With greater difficulty, feet can be held together as they reach out. (2) Arch to each side, to front, and to the rear which is the most difficult, particularly the return from being well arched back. (3) Stand-ing with feet wide apart allows you to reach to all sides.

**Arms**

An arc of space, in a semi-circle, hands at centre; straight lines towards and back from hands; jumping feet to space between or out-side of hands; bunny jumps into a low space above head; handstand into high space above head.

## APPARATUS WORK

**Climbing frames** Bench is hooked high on to a bar so that it is steeply inclined for travel-ling up, under or around. **Ropes, mats** (1) Emphasise transfer to a grip with both hands together, from a position with feet firmly crossed. (2) Legs can swing hanging low; angled at a medium horizontal; or hooked high above hands on rope. **Trestles** (1) 'Near to' circling, sliding, crawling, hanging under with arms and legs wrapped round. (2) 'High balance' on one foot, on tip toes, sitting astride, high kneeling, upended on shoulders.

**Bench, upturned bench, trestle, mats** (1) 'Low balances' on all fours, on one hand and one foot, sitting, side towards on one hand and one foot. (2) 'Tall balances' on tip toes, one foot, shoulders. **Boxes, mats** High, wide shaped jumps up and from apparatus. **Mats** The small, slow forward roll can be from a starting, crouch position, reaching down to just in front of feet. The bigger roll can be longer and quicker with a dive to lift you momentarily off the floor, over an imaginary obstacle.

## FINAL FLOOR ACTIVITY

The floor patterns that lend themselves to work on the spot, then work in the whole room space, include circles, triangles, straight line corridors, figures of eight.

## LESSON PLAN • 30–35 MINUTES

### LESSON THEME

Good use of effort to achieve controlled performance: we are concerned with the degree of force being applied, and the amount of speed being used.

### FLOORWORK                                              12–15 minutes

**Legs** (1) Run with a relaxed, 'easy' action that feels effortless. (2) Now, change between slow running when you have little space, and quick running when there is plenty of room. (3) Can you link together an easy, soft jump on the spot; slow running; then a quick run into an explosive, upward jump?
**Body** (1) From a still standing position, lower to sitting and rock smoothly back on to shoulders and hands. Balance still, then rock back to standing, building up speed for a strong spring up on to feet. (2) A variation could be a start, balanced on one foot with the other leg and both arms stretched well forward, before your very slow lower to sitting. Your speedy return, if powerful enough, could take you up on to one foot only, again.
**Arms** (1) Can you hold a handstand for three seconds, using spread fingers strongly to control you? (2) In how many ways can you come down, softly, under control? (3) If you prefer, show me your longest, slowest ever cartwheel.

### APPARATUS WORK                                         16–18 minutes

**Climbing frames** Travel in many directions, using two hands then two feet. Can you include moments when your whole body is being supported by your hands? **Boxes, mats** (1) Can you plan a sequence to include favourite activities across box and along long return box? Include good gymnastic links between the lines. (2) Make your work even more interesting by showing a contrast in speed or force applied. **Trestles** (1) Start and finish on the floor. Show ways to mount on to the apparatus, using arms or legs strongly. (2) Use your hands strongly to return you gently to the floor. **Mats** (1) Revise cartwheel, emphasising firm, stretched body position and four long counts of hand, hand, foot, foot. (2) At return mats, practise a forward roll to standing with one foot behind the other. Swivel body round to side of rear foot and finish with a backward roll. **Ropes** Revise leading-up stages to rope climbing as appropriate for each child. (a) Swing freely on rope, practising hands together grip. (b) Swing from sitting on a chair to let you secure a strong, crossed foot grip. (c) Swing from standing and try to take one hand off to prove a strong foot grip. (d) Climb. Hand; hand; hands together; feet up. **Benches, mats** From a position on the cross bench, can you transfer slowly to the mats, making your hands important? At the return cross bench, show a lively, contrasting movement where your legs are important.

### FINAL FLOOR ACTIVITY                                        2 minutes

Walk, run, jump and land where feet land one after the other, gradually slowing to a still finish.

## NC requirements being emphasised

(a) Emphasising changes of speed and effort through gymnastic actions.
(b) Making appropriate decisions quickly and planning their responses.

## FLOORWORK

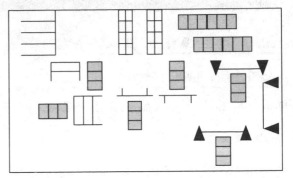

**Legs** (1) When we apply effort and body tension, we can 'feel' how we are moving. We want to feel so easy that we could keep on going. (2) Slow running, including running on the spot if necessary to avoid others, is accompanied by a lowering of arms and heels and an upright body. In quicker running, we incline forward more and lift heels, knees and arms more for the rapid striding. (3) Gentle effort; slow motion; accelerating motion into maximum effect are all represented and asked for in this sequence.

**Body** (1) The build up of speed to rock you back from shoulder balance to standing is helped by a vigorous, strong leg swing. (2) Variety in return from shoulder balance include a slight change of direction, and coming up on to one foot or to feet crossed.

**Arms** (1) A good hand balance starts with just the right amount of arms and leg swing to take you up. We have to practise and remember how it feels when it is just right. (2) The soft, gentle return to standing contrasts with the strong firm push up. (3) Slow work on hands, all looking neat and well controlled, is our aim – plus the excellent physical demands being made on arms and shoulder muscles.

## APPARATUS WORK

**Climbing frames** Particularly when supported by hands only, keep both thumbs gripping under the bars, fingers over, for a safe, strong hold. **Boxes, mats** (1) Make work non-stop by including jumps, rolls or cartwheels between the two lines, rather than just walking between. (2) Work on hands and rolls can be slow. Jumps can be dynamic. **Trestles** (1) Strong hand action is needed to grip and hang below; or push to lift up and on; to grip sides and pull along; to circle round and on to; to twist across or on. (2) Leave, using hands as you circle round pole; as you roll from sitting or kneeling; as you bunny jump off; as you twist from. **Mats** (1) Even if cartwheel is diagonal to floor, rather than vertical, a firm, stretched body can be demonstrated. (2) Shoulder above crossed behind foot swings round into the turn. **Ropes** Emphasise hands together grip when pulling both feet up to their next, crossed feet together grip. **Benches** Slow, strong hands contrast with sudden, explosive legs.

## FINAL FLOOR ACTIVITY

Accelerate into the jump and try to decelerate on landing, to a still finish position.

## LESSON PLAN • 30–35 MINUTES

### LESSON THEME

Revision and direct teaching of simple, traditional gymnastic skills.

### FLOORWORK                                      13–16 minutes

**Legs** (1) Using three running steps, only, each time, run and jump up with a stretch, a (wide) star and a tuck, moving on a triangular pathway. (2) Stand. Do a jump up and a half-turn, swinging one arm across to create the turn. Right arm swings when jumping up and turning to the left.
**Body** (1) Stand, balanced on one leg, with upper body inclined well forward, arms upstretched, and other leg stretched well back. (2) Lower back and down to balance sitting with head up, legs straight and together, and arms stretched sideways for balance. (Seat only on floor.) (3) Rock back to shoulder balance with legs straight and together. Hands can either support hips at rear, or press hard down on floor. (4) Swing back up to standing and repeat.
**Arms** We have been doing our handstands and cartwheels from a standing position. Try to co-ordinate a two or three step run into either or both. The extra momentum will help you to invert more easily and quickly.

### APPARATUS WORK                                 17–19 minutes

**Mats** Try to link together two of your favourite agilities. **Climbing frames** Rotary descent from top bars. Sit at top, with hands crossed on bar at face height. One hand grips with knuckles towards you, the other grips with knuckles away from you. Lower your body by twisting the shoulder of the near hand (knuckles towards you) backwards. You will lower, turning, to the bar below. **Ropes** (1) Circle backwards, gripping two ropes at shoulder height, by lifting both legs up and over head. (2) Reverse hanging on two ropes. Hands at shoulder height, lift legs up and off floor to stretch them up towards ceiling, or hook one leg round each rope. **Upturned benches, mats** (1) On parallel benches, balance walk with some contact with a partner. (2) On mats, practise going from elbow balance into a bent leg headstand. **Boxes, mats** Cat spring on to end of long box top. Either cat spring, roll, cartwheel or vault off the other end. At cross box, face vault or gate vault over. 'Face vault' is like a high bunny jump and you twist over, facing box top, all the way. 'Gate vault' has hands facing forward, legs lift straight to one side as they come round and down, with hand on swinging side lifting off. **Trestles** Circle up and down on metal pole. Roll from planks on to mats. Upward jumps with half-turns from planks.

### FINAL FLOOR ACTIVITY                           2 minutes

Start at the back of the room. Run forward to opposite end, and do your three starting jumps before reaching the other end. Turn, and we will all go back again.

## NC requirements being emphasised

(a) Responding readily to instructions.
(b) Sustaining energetic activity and working vigorously to develop suppleness and strength and to exercise the heart and lungs strongly.

## FLOORWORK

**Legs** (1) 'Good things happen in threes' and a triangle of jumps brings you back to own starting place. Runs are short, about 3 metres. Jumps are the main thing. (2) Four jumps on the spot facing forward can be followed by two, each of which includes a quarter turn. Four more on the spot, then two with a quarter turn to bring you back to start.
**Body** (1) First position is called horizontal balance standing. (2) The sitting balance has the body tilted back slightly with a strong effort to keep back, arms and legs all stretched. (3) Feet with stretched ankles should be above hips, which should be above shoulders, all in a line, balanced on shoulders. (4) Legs swing strongly, then bend under you to take you standing.
**Arms** This walk and skip with one leg and both arms swinging up together can lead into a handstand practice on the floor, against a wall, or against the supporting teacher.

## APPARATUS WORK

**Mats** You can show your work to a partner who will tell you what he or she liked, and one way in which you can improve. Partner might ask for clearer shapes and neater, still start and finish. **Climbing frames** Strong arm and shoulder exercise with strong abdominal exercise as you lift your legs to twist down each time. Momentarily, all body weight is supported by arms but tummy muscles work hard to lift seat and legs clear of bar. **Ropes** (1) Shoulder height grip important to ensure feet come down to floor again, and not left dangling in mid-air. Bent, short lever legs easier to lift into circle than straight legs. (2) Let them choose to hook feet round ropes, or try to hold them straight together, away from ropes. **Upturned benches, mats** (1) Walk facing each other; side by side; facing opposite directions, hand in hand, hand on shoulder. (2) Legs are bent in elbow balance, from which you lower slowly on to forehead and hands. **Boxes, mats** Face vault much easier than gate vault. **Trestles** The attractive variety from rolls, circles and jumps is worth demonstrating, particularly if virtually non-stop with a good group, sharing, thinking ahead and never queuing.

## FINAL FLOOR ACTIVITY

Run and jump stretched, run and jump wide, run and jump tucked.

## LESSON PLAN • 30–35 MINUTES

### LESSON THEME

Partner work with emphasis on matching and contrasting movements. Observing, copying or contrasting a partner's movement develops one's powers of observation and an awareness of the elements of movement.

### FLOORWORK                                                    12–15 minutes

**Legs** One behind other, about 1¹/₂ metres apart, the leader travels on feet and then stops. At each re-start, a slight change of direction, body shape or speed is introduced in the next travel and stop and the actions can change.
**Body** With other partner now as leader, the couples face each other. Start in a half-kneeling position on one lower leg and the opposite hand. In your three or four balance sequence, use a variety of supporting parts and interesting linking movements.
**Arms** 'A' makes various bridges, supported strongly on hands and feet. 'B' travels under, over, through or around 'A', using hands and feet only as supports. Change over duties.

### APPARATUS WORK                                               16–18 minutes

**Climbing frames** Can you show me ways of travelling over, under and around each other?
**Upturned benches** (1) On the parallel upturned benches, keep some contact with your partner as you balance forward, sideways or backwards. (2) Support your partner in a bent leg headstand. **Ropes** Using ropes, floor and mats, can you plan a matching sequence, done together? **Trestles** Start at opposite sides or ends of the apparatus. Approach, meet, negotiate each other, finish in partner's starting place. **Cross bench, mats** Starting at opposite sides, can you build up to a matching approach, flight and landing?
**Boxes, mats** Watch your partner's sequence which includes a jump, a roll and taking all the weight on hands at some point. While your partner practises, improves and remembers his or her sequence, can you, the observer, create a contrasting sequence? (For example, different shape in the jump; a roll in the opposite direction, or at a different speed; weight on hands with a different leg shape or action.)

### FINAL FLOOR ACTIVITY                                         2 minutes

Side by side, jump up on the spot; run three steps into a high matching jump and identical landing; jump up into a half-turn and repeat.

## NC requirements being emphasised

(a) Working safely, alone and with others.
(b) Developing skill by exploring and making up activities and by expressing themselves imaginatively.

## FLOORWORK

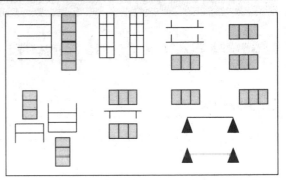

**Legs** Because there has to be a travel and a stop, the following, copying partner can stand still, observing and remembering the action, and then catch up with the leader each time. The challenge for the observer is to recognise the nature of the 'slight change' each time, and, of course, for the leader to put one in. If using demonstrations here, ask the observers 'What changes did you see?'

**Body** The new leader is asked for a variety of supporting parts and slow, smooth linking movements. Emphasise that it is a balance sequence, requiring difficulty in holding the balance on a small or unusual body part or parts. Good pairs, mirroring each other in exact unison, deserve to be presented for a demonstration.

**Arms** Both partners are to be supported on hands and feet, with the stationary partner sufficiently high and arched to leave room for travelling by the partner. 'A' can bridge with front, back or side to the floor and change bridges to give partner a new challenge to negotiate.

## APPARATUS WORK

**Climbing frames** One partner can stay and work in centre four spaces while other travels across, around, under or over him or her. **Upturned benches** (1) They can face opposite ways to travel; touch each other with different body parts (hands, elbows, hand to shoulder, hands to shoulders), and show same or contrasting shapes. (2) Supporting partner kneels in front of partner, lifting hips and back against own chest as partner walks in and lifts to headstand. **Ropes** Aim for a matching stationary start; then a matching side by side travel (e.g. swing and forward roll, or swing and cartwheel); then a still, matching finish.

**Trestles** At the point of 'negotiation', one can be stationary while the other travels under, over or past him or her. **Cross bench, mats** A starting signal by one partner can be a little lifting of heels by one, signifying 'Now!' (Let's go!) **Boxes, mats** The elements to consider in planning for contrast are: shape; direction; speed; and different uses of body parts. (For example, a diving, stretched roll forwards, done vigorously to contrast with a sideways, tightly curled roll, slowly and easily.) This difficult challenge needs good observation and planning.

## FINAL FLOOR ACTIVITY

Couples work, side by side, or one slightly ahead, back and forward, in a narrow corridor, only 3–4 metres in length. The starting signal can be a slight knees bend by the leader, just before the jump.

# Year 6 • July • Lesson 11

## LESSON PLAN • 30–35 MINUTES

### LESSON THEME

Sequences, through which the children work harder for longer, expressing vigour, skilfulness, understanding and, it is hoped, enthusiasm, enjoyment and satisfaction.

### FLOORWORK 12–15 minutes

**Legs** Show me a sequence where you work on the spot to start with, then travel to a new space of your own. Can you plan to include more than one kind of leg action, and examples of both gentle and vigorous movements?
**Body** Including a lunge among your stretches, can you travel using stretching and curling movements? Working at different levels, using different supporting parts, will provide interesting variety.
**Arms** Travel, using feet and hands where you emphasise the varied pattern of possible foot and hand movements. They can move alternately; left side only; right side only; apart; together; or run and cartwheel or handstand, etc.

### APPARATUS WORK 16–18 minutes

**Climbing frames** (1) Using floor and apparatus, can you balance, travel, balance using a variety of supporting parts in your balances? (2) Can you plan to include being vertical, horizontal and upended? **Ropes** (1) In your climbing emphasise the full stretch after the three count hand shift, and the full curl after the high leg lift. (2) Show me a sequence of three swings that include a change of direction, speed and body shape. **Inverted benches, mats** In your balancing along the benches, travel at different levels and include a change of direction somewhere. At the mats, revise elbow balance and/or bent leg headstand. **Boxes, mats** Can you include a rolling action along the low long box and mats? Show me a vaulting action with shoulders over hands on the return cross box. Try to plan for a long flowing sequence with neat links between the lines. **Trestles, planks, pole, mats** Can you travel, using all the apparatus, with feet leading or following on, under, across, around and along the apparatus? **Mats** Show me a balance, roll, balance sequence where you include at least one upended balance and a change of direction somewhere. At the return mats can you do a forward roll followed by a dive forward roll (i.e. whole of body in air at one point)?

### FINAL FLOOR ACTIVITY 2 minutes

Using legs only, make up a sequence of walking, running and jumping which includes varied actions in flight. For example: hurdling; jacknife; scissors; tuck; rolling one leg over the other.

## NC requirements being emphasised

(a) Making appropriate decisions quickly and planning their responses.
(b) Practising, adapting, improving and repeating longer and increasingly complex sequences of movement.
(c) Making judgements and suggesting ways to improve.

## TEACHING POINTS

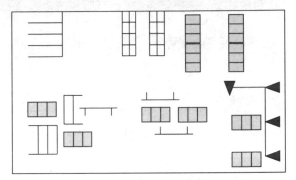

These sequences and performances show the level of skilfulness, knowledge, understanding and attitudes that have developed during the four years of the Gymnastic Activities course.

### Skills

(1) The ability to plan, perform, remember and refine a series of movements into a pleasing, varied sequence which answers the task.
(2) The ability to demonstrate control, poise, vigour and versatility in sequences which make full use of all 'movement' elements.

### Knowledge and understanding

(1) Awareness of the 'movement' elements that influence quality and aesthetic appeal in gymnastic performances – variety, contrast, repetition, body tension and clarity of shape.
(2) Understanding how to apply these movement elements to the parts of a sequence to make the performance more demanding, and more interesting and satisfying to performer and spectator.

### Desirable class attitudes

'What you don't use, you lose. We, the class, have continually been taught and encouraged to develop and make full use of our strength, stamina, suppleness and versatility.

These lessons have been good fun, exciting and food for us. We believe that they have made us very fit because of the way the whole body is being exercised so strongly. We also believe that you look and feel better if you exercise regularly.

Working with others; learning with them and from them; giving and receiving demonstrations; and hearing their friendly, encouraging comments have all made these lessons particularly sociable and friendly and brought our class together in a special way.

Our teacher has said that we will be remembered for our wholehearted, co-operative, enthusiastic responses, neat, well controlled, versatile, high quality work, and our capacity for working hard to achieve success.'

## LESSON PLAN • 30–35 MINUTES

### LESSON THEME

Re-establishing good habits in working quietly, vigorously and thoughtfully, and responding immediately to the teacher's requests. Sensible sharing of space.

### FLOORWORK                                                    12–15 minutes

**Legs** (1) Can you show me ways of travelling and stopping, travelling and stopping? Look for a space before going. (2) Varied leg actions might include 'easy', slow and vigorous, lively, difficult to stop actions. (3) Use arms well to balance you, both in your travelling and stopping.
**Body** (1) Balance, stretched on shoulders. Swing one or both legs to take you into your next balanced position. Swing part or parts of you to move again. (2) Stretch strongly those parts not supporting you. Use a swing each time to start the move. (3) Can you plan to include different levels for variety?
**Arms** (1) Can you cartwheel, handstand or bunny jump to take you from feet to hands to feet? (2) Can you show stillness between each action, and make one finishing position become the starting position for the following action?

### APPARATUS WORK                                               16–18 minutes

**Climbing frames** (1) Climb up on any pathway you choose, head leading. Come down, feet leading. (2) Revise sitting, cross hands grip, rotary descent. One hand grips with knuckles towards you, one grips with knuckles away from you. Lower by twisting to sit on the next bar down, facing the opposite way. Twist by pulling shoulder of near hand backwards. **Ropes** Climb partially up one rope and transfer across several ropes. Use strong hands together and crossed feet actions between shifts. **Trestles** Using apparatus or apparatus and floor, show a clear body shape as you travel on to, across, along, under, around and from the apparatus. **Cross bench, mats** At the cross bench demonstrate ways to go into a roll. At return mats show me two favourite agilities neatly linked. **Boxes, bench** Use your hands to bring you on to the boxes each time. At return long bench, can you use your feet only? In some way can you demonstrate a contrast between the box and the bench work? **Cross bench, mats** Cross the bench in one direction, using the bench as a spring board for a vigorous drive up and forward. Cross the bench the other way without touching it and with a more gentle, flowing action.

### FINAL FLOOR ACTIVITY                                         2 minutes

Lie, stretched out on back. Two complete rolls to one side with body stretched. Curl up tightly on back, hands clasped under knees; roll completely sideways twice, back to starting place.

## NC requirements being emphasised

(a) Planning longer sequences, able to envisage the finished product, and showing aesthetic qualities, including variety, contrast and repetition.

(b) Being physically active.

## FLOORWORK

**Legs** (1) Be still, travel, be still, emphasises the beginning, middle, end of pieces of work being a pattern and a complete whole. (2) Variety and contrast are highlighted at start of the year. Varied uses of effort, speed, actions, plus 'poised neatness', all contribute to the 'aesthetic quality' of the work. (3) Arms balance you in flight and on landing; they can swing you up into a jump; and they contribute to clear shapes and neat work.

**Body** (1) All start in same, inverted balance, then plan to move on to other supporting parts with the help of a swing each time. (2) Parts 'not supporting' usually include an arm and/or a leg. (3) As we move from low, through medium, up to high, we tend to use less and less supporting parts in our still balances.

**Arms** (1) A triangle of actions is recommended to bring you back to your starting place, as you go from feet only to hands only, back to feet only, ready for the next example. (2) Planning ahead is necessary to arrange for the end of one to be the start of the next activity.

## APPARATUS WORK

**Climbing frames** (1) Emphasise the thumbs under, fingers over grip on bars for a safe, strong, unslipping hold. (2) Revision of rotary descent will be a welcome reminder and challenge to this skills enthusiastic age group. Their pursuit of strength and fitness will also be served in this most difficult arm, shoulder and abdominal muscles exercise. **Ropes** This lends itself to a follow the leader piece of partner work, one of many partner examples suddenly presenting themselves. **Trestles** Quality is being demonstrated in the repertoire of ways of travelling that each group presents, and in the beautifully clear, firm body shapes being emphasised. **Cross benches, mats** Group members can demonstrate the simpler rolls; then the run and jump rolls; then standing dive to running dive forward rolls as a progression, with teacher assistance. **Boxes, benches** 'Contrast' in directions, speed or level, for example. **Cross bench, mats** Non-stop action with some gymnastic link at the end of each part, rather than just walking to face next bench.

## FINAL FLOOR ACTIVITY

Impetus for straight body rolls comes from the opposite leg or shoulder swinging across. Impetus for the curled up sideways roll comes from a swing of knees and hands.

## LESSON PLAN • 30–35 MINUTES

### LESSON THEME

Development of quality and variety in natural body activities and movements, with a particular emphasis on good use of feet and hands.

### FLOORWORK                                           12–15 minutes

**Legs**  Practise a group of skip jumps on the spot, stretching ankles fully (i.e. 'pointed toes') and then run into a jump and a beautifully balanced finish where feet and arm positions are very interesting.
**Body**  (1) In a sequence of rolling, balancing and twisting movements, can you let your arms or legs be the parts that lead you into and out of the various movements?  (2) Let the roundness of your rolls contrast with the stretch of parts not supporting you in your balances.
**Arms**  Can you use a swinging action with hand or hands, leg or legs, or hand and leg to take all your weight on to your hands?

### APPARATUS WORK                                      16–18 minutes

**Climbing frames**  With the emphasis on a strong arm action, travel over both frames, bench and mats. How often can you be completely supported by your arms? **Ropes** (1) Using two ropes, can you swing legs to hang upside down with legs stretched or hooked round two ropes? (2) Can you circle feet from floor overhead to floor, using two ropes? **Trestles**  As you travel show me the different supporting or gripping actions that help you best as you cross, circle round, pull along above or below, lever on to, swing or slide on the various apparatus surfaces. **Upturned benches, trestle, mats**  (1) Balance walk on bench, keeping some part of both feet in constant contact with the bench. (2) Cat walk balance along bench, crouched on hands and feet, with hips low and knees well bent. (3) At mats and trestle show me balances where the hands are the most important parts in contrast to the important feet on the benches. **Boxes, mats**  Use hands strongly to bring you on to the boxes. (Lever roll, vault, twist.) Use legs strongly to take you off. **Mats**  Try a cartwheeling action along one line of mats. Try rolling actions with a variety of leg and arm positions back along the other mats.

### FINAL FLOOR ACTIVITY                                 2 minutes

(1) Swing into upward jump on the spot; run and swing into high jump. (2) Let beautifully stretched arms, balancing you throughout, be matched by neat, quiet, foot actions.

# LESSON NOTES • 4–5 LESSONS DEVELOPMENT

## NC requirement being emphasised

Increasing their range of skills and adapting and refining performance.

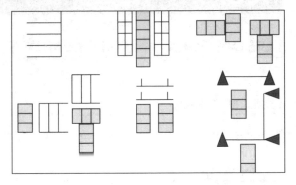

## FLOORWORK

**Legs** Jumps on the spot alternate with a short run into a jump emphasising quality from a firm body tension at every stage, in particular the well balanced (proud?) finish, which becomes the place from which to repeat the work, adjusting to the new space.

**Body** (1) For example, a simple log roll with body stretched, twisting from back to back again; a swing up of legs to shoulder balance; a twist to lower legs back over shoulder to kneeling. (2) For example, back lying, curled up small; roll sideways right over on to front; change to balance on one hand and one knee, stretching the non-supporting hand and leg strongly; twist to roll along one arm on to back to start again.

**Arms** Swinging as an inspiration to moving into and out of a position is worth practising for its own sake. We use it often, unwittingly. Here we are helping the pupils see how it helps to move us.

## APPARATUS WORK

**Climbing frames** Thumbs under bar and fingers over is important for a safe, strong grip. Try to be 'wholly supported' as you hang, lower from hanging, lift into circling round a bar, lift into a rotary descent to next bar down. **Ropes** (1) Grasp rope at shoulder height with bent arms to ensure that feet return to floor after hanging upside down. Feet can be hooked round a rope or together, stretched upwards. (2) A bent legs, short lever lift into the circle is easier than a straight leg lift. **Trestles** Variety in hand actions is worth demonstrating because good hands contribute so much to body management in gymnastic activities as they lever on to; circle round; hang and pull; swing to off; vault over.

**Upturned benches, trestle, mats** Good quality balancing will include a still, non-wobbling firmness, with its non-supporting parts beautifully stretched. High level balancing is the more difficult. **Boxes, mats** Timing of walk, skip or run and take-off on to hands is as important as the run into jump at the start of the lesson. A preparatory swing of one leg or one of both arms helps the strong leg action from the apparatus. **Mats** Aim to have hand, hand, foot, foot as near to a straight line as possible. 'One, two or no hands in your rolls' is a good challenge.

## FINAL FLOOR ACTIVITY

Can be done, progressing all round room, or back and forward in your own, narrow corridor, with short runs.

## LESSON PLAN • 30–35 MINUTES

### LESSON THEME

Balancing with stress on body parts and apparatus on which a balance can be held.

### FLOORWORK                                                          12–15 minutes

**Legs** (1) Run a few steps, jump and turn to one side. Experiment with arm positions and leg actions and positions to see which helps your landing into balance the most. (2) Stand on one foot and slowly take one foot off the ground. Stretch the raised leg in various directions, forwards, sideways and backwards. Move your upper body and arms to maintain balance. Change to balancing on other foot.

**Body** In a sequence of bridge-like shapes, can you make your positions more difficult to hold by reducing the number of supporting parts and stretching strongly the parts not being used?

**Arms** Can you hold a handstand balance for 3 seconds?

### APPARATUS WORK                                                     16–18 minutes

(1) Run all round the room, making jumps into half-turn landings, showing a good balance position in arms and legs. Use floor and mats only.
(2) Keep working and when I call 'Stop!' show me a bridge on the nearest piece of apparatus. Make it difficult by using the least possible number of supporting parts. Stop! (3) **Climbing frames** Travel, using hands and feet going up, across, diagonally and through. Show me a balance in between different actions and directions. **Ropes** (1) Balanced partly on floor and partly on rope, can you show me a bridge-like shape? (2) Can you run and swing strongly, letting go at the end of the swing, to land in a well-balanced position?

**Trestles** Aim for group variety by showing the varied parts of the apparatus and yourselves on which balances can be held. **Upturned benches, mats** Try mounting to balance standing on benches, then travelling along using feet or feet and hands. At the mats can you balance with your feet above your head? **Boxes, mats** From a beautifully balanced starting position on tip toes, run up to and on to the box top. On the box show a balance on one foot, moving upper body and arms to help balance you. Leave with an upward jump and run to your next starting point. **Mats** Revise the floorwork sequence of three bridge-like balances at different levels on different supporting parts.

### FINAL FLOOR ACTIVITY                                               2 minutes

Stand; lift one straight leg forward; lower to sitting and roll back to shoulder balance; rock back to starting position.

# LESSON NOTES • 4–5 LESSONS DEVELOPMENT

## NC requirements being emphasised

(a) Refining and increasing range of balancing skills, including the ability to move fluently into and out of balance.

(b) Understanding the factors which influence quality, including extension, body tension and clarity of body shape.

## FLOORWORK

**Legs** (1) The jump to turn to one side will be helped by a swing of opposite arm or leg to that side. Landing with one foot arriving on the floor after the other slows you down easily. Arms stretched to front or side help the balance. (2) Explain that 'balance' means we are on some small or unusual part of our body, and that we have to work hard to avoid wobbling about, to hold a neat, still, steady balance position. We can add to the difficulty in balancing by moving the upper body quite far, while on the one foot.

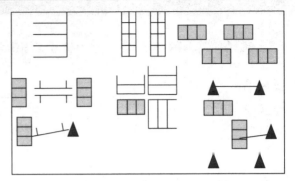

**Body** An interesting balance challenge is 'Can you make a sequence of three, still stretched balances, going down from three to two to only one point of support?' in addition to the example given.

**Arms** Horizontal legs (one forward, one held back) help balance.

## APPARATUS WORK

**Climbing frames** Challenge whole group to show a variety of supporting body parts, at different heights including using floor and frames, to show off to class. **Ropes** (1) Bridge-like can be standing, sitting, lying, side towards floor on one hand and one foot, while holding rope in some way. (2) Let go with one hand as feet touch floor. Land, helped to balance with one hand grip on rope. Balanced well, take second hand away from rope. **Trestles** Group variety again is the challenge to inspire variety and to extend the class' (and the teacher's) repertoire. **Upturned benches,**

**mats** Stand astride bench with hands on balance surface and feet on floor. Lift one foot at a time to place it on balance surface. When both feet are on, stand after lowering back on to both feet from your crouched position. **Boxes, mats** 'On to box top' can be by way of a roll, a high jump or a vault with hands on, then on to feet to standing. **Mats** Performing on a mat lets you include more adventurous balances and linking movements. For example, headstand and handstand bridges (arch behind knees) and rolls to new supporting parts.

## FINAL FLOOR ACTIVITY

A five part, interesting and varied sequence at different levels and with some good ideas for linking movements between the positions.

## LESSON PLAN • 30–35 MINUTES

### LESSON THEME

Revision and direct teaching of some of the traditional gymnastic skills.

### FLOORWORK                                                13–16 minutes

**Legs** (1) Practise four skip jumps to face each of the four walls. (2) Practise four skip jumps travelling a short distance forward, to the right, backwards and to the left, back to starting position.
**Body** (1) From a standing position, lunge well forward with a long step and bend of one leg. Arms are stretched parallel above head and stretched rear leg is up on toes. Bent knee of lunging leg is over foot. (2) Rear leg is brought up beside the forward, lunging leg and you return to standing. Next time, lunge forward with other foot.
**Arms** (1) Front support position on hands and feet on floor with hands and feet about shoulder width apart. Spring whole body up and off floor at same time. (2) Bunny jump position on floor, crouched with hands on floor shoulder width apart. Keep feet together and lift them off floor a few inches and lower two or three times before a strong kick up behind of both feet up into handstand.

### APPARATUS WORK                                           17–19 minutes

**Climbing frames** Sitting on one bar. Horizontal travelling to one side to next space, facing opposite way. Going to right, place right hand under next space bar, with thumb towards you and knuckles away from you. Start pulling strongly to right and twisting into the next space. At same time reach across with left hand to place it on bar along from left hand, with knuckles on same side. Both arms pull strongly to bring you to sitting on the next bar. **Ropes, benches, mats** Pendulum action swings from bench to mats or back to bench. Start off with a strong jump upwards and backwards from the bench to create the extra swing length to bring you back to the bench easily. **Mats** Forward rolls. Crouch, chin on chest, head well tucked in. Roll with a strong push from legs. At end of roll, with body still tucked, heels are pulled in near to seat, arms are reaching forward. Backward rolls. Sit, seat close to heels, hands ready at shoulders. Rounded back, chin on chest, hands flat on floor, thumbs nearest to ears. Strong push with arms back on to feet. **Boxes, mats** Face vault or gate vault over cross box top. Two hands on box, twist across in face vault, facing box all the way. **Mats** Handstand, forward roll; or elbow balance into bent leg headstand.

### FINAL FLOOR ACTIVITY                                      2 minutes

Can you do three skip jumps on the spot, then a choice of a favourite tucked, jacknifed or twisted jump?

## NC requirement being emphasised

Refining and increasing range of gymnastic actions involving flight, swinging, and lifting and lowering the body.

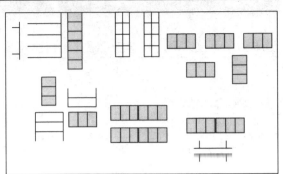

## FLOORWORK

**Legs** (1) Contrast body tension in body in flight with the soft, 'give' of ankles and knees on landing. Can they keep repeating the rhythm? (2) Look out for and comment on any excellent, strong, supple ankle actions. Many will be stiff and not stretching satisfactorily. One of many reasons for barefoot work is to see how ankles are working in activities such as this.

**Body** (1) As well as being a strong exercise for the front, supporting leg this is a strong exercise for the back and shoulders muscles, particularly with the long lever of the upstretched arms. (2) Recovery from lunge can be to crouch with legs bent. Lunge can be turned to face alternate sides, foot still going forwards, or you can lunge to one side over supporting leg.

**Arms** (1) Bounce comes from slight lowering of hips followed by a swing up of hips. (2) As well as bunny jumps into handstand, you can lever up on to hands from a crouch, without the jump.

## APPARATUS WORK

**Climbing frames** Horizontal travel is a very strong movement in arms, shoulders and abdominals in lifting through to next space. Recite 'Undergrasp, overgrasp, head through, and pull.' **Ropes, benches, mats** Challenge group 'Can you make two swings and still land back on the bench or mat where you started?' This is only possible after a superb backward jump, away from the target, to create the long pendulum. Hands should be high enough to stop you hitting floor at bottom of swing. **Mats** Emphasise one touch only on floor in forward roll. (No second touch to push you up to standing.) At end of backward roll, can you push from being on shoulders to right up on to feet, not knees? **Boxes, mats** Face vault is easier because both hands stay on box top, like a high bunny jump, as your body twists round, still facing the box, to the other side. In gate vault, straight legs need to swing straight to the side where no hand is supporting, and the body faces forward all the time. **Mats** Three listed are in decreasing order of difficulty.

## FINAL FLOOR ACTIVITY

Three, then the 'favourite' one which needs good height to be achieved.

# Year 7 • January • Lesson 5

## LESSON PLAN • 30–35 MINUTES

### LESSON THEME

Body shape awareness with a particular emphasis on the contribution that a clear, controlled body shape makes to the look and the difficulty of a movement.

### FLOORWORK                                                    12–15 minutes

**Legs** (1) Take up a starting shape. Run and jump to show the same shape in flight. (2) Can you repeat and then move on to a different shape?
**Body** (1) Kneeling, with knees apart and feet together, can you arch your body sideways, forward and backwards, producing good body shapes? (2) Use your arms well to improve the look of the arches and try to link the arches together with interesting movements.
**Arms** (1) Revise cartwheels where the body shape remains constant during the movement. (2) As a contrast, can you show me a way to change body shape while moving on hands?

### APPARATUS WORK                                               16–18 minutes

**Climbing frames** Using floor and apparatus can you demonstrate ways of travelling that involve the body in long, wide, rounded or twisted shapes? **Ropes** Revise rope climbing with the emphasis on a strong upward jump to reach hands as high as possible to start with, then lift feet up as high as possible to secure their first crossed foot grip. Then the three hand movements. One hand, other hand, first hand up past and next to second hand, then the strong pull up of legs again. Three hand shifts take body to a full stretch position. **Trestles** On, around, suspended from the various apparatus and surrounding floor, can you arch your body forward, sideways, backwards? **Benches, box** Try to 'feel' your whole body shape in your vigorous actions up to, along, over or from the apparatus. **Bench, box, mats** Can you cross bench, box or mats keeping leg or legs straight? You can make legs or hands or both important in supporting you. **Mats** Revise the kneeling arching forward, sideways or backwards that we did in the floorwork. Try some other supporting parts that are good on the mat (e.g. back of head and heels; kneels and elbows; side of one shoulder and one foot; bent leg headstand).

### FINAL FLOOR ACTIVITY                                         2 minutes

Travel freely round room, changing shape every three or four seconds. For example, skipping, straight legs; running with knees bent; bouncing with feet wide astride and arms stretched out.

## NC requirements being emphasised

**(a)** Being taught to understand the factors which influence quality in performances, including body tension and clear body shape.
**(b)** Understanding and assessing how well they and others have achieved what they set out to do.

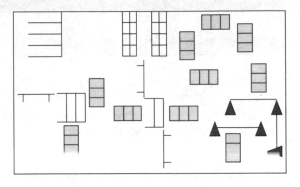

## FLOORWORK

**Legs** (1) The run is 3–4 metres short because the jump is the main activity. All shapes are possible at start and in flight. We can stand stretched, wide, arched, twisted, tucked (knees bent, crouched), and even in a jacknife with upper body reaching down. (2) A two-footed take-off is recommended for maximum height to allow time for an excellent jump plus clear shape.

**Body** (1) Let the movement be a slow curl into the arch, starting at the top and moving down the spine. Form the curled position, return to being stretched by unrolling from the bottom upwards. (2) Long arms starting above head enhance and magnify the arch, but also make the body work harder because of the extra leverage.

**Arms** (1) Whether done with an expert, vertical performance, or a lower diagonal to the floor, beginner's performance, the wide star shape of the ideal cartwheel should be the aim.
(2) While on hands you can vary leg positions to a long stretch, a wide star, to bent, to one stretched and one bent.

## APPARATUS WORK

**Climbing frames** Hands climb up to full stretch. Feet follow to tight curl. Sideways can be from star shape to pencil shape, wide to narrow. Weave by curling through spaces, stretch to climb. **Ropes** One hand up, other hand up, hands together, pull feet up, with emphasis on strong pull up being with hands together. **Trestles** The arch shape can be supported on tummy, hanging from back of knees, on hands and feet, on shoulders and heels. **Benches, box** 'Vigorous' means lots of runs and jumps on to and over; lots of dynamic springs up and from feet, hands support across, rolls. **Bench, box, mats** Straight leg rolls, vaults, cartwheels, running jumps. **Mats** Variety from being upright, upended or with front, back or one side to the floor.

## FINAL FLOOR ACTIVITY

The combined change of action and change of shape is a good challenge to their ability to plan ahead.

## LESSON PLAN • 30–35 MINUTES

### LESSON THEME

Partner work and exploring ways to work with someone else to create movements that are impossible when working individually.

### FLOORWORK — 12–15 minutes

**Legs** One partner demonstrates skip jumping on the spot. The other partner watches, 'feels' the timing of the jumps, and then starts jumping up as partner is coming down.
**Body** (1) Near each other, partners hold a tight, curled position on own choice of body parts. Both slowly uncurl, to a firm, fully stretched position where there is contact made between partners. (2) Return, curling, joint by joint, to starting, curled position.
**Arms** Show your partner your way of going up to and trying to hold a handstand, or do a handwalk. Your partner will watch your demonstration, and then tell you what they liked about it, and one way in which it can be improved.

### APPARATUS WORK — 16–18 minutes

(1) Follow your leader, touching floor only, in a short walk, and a short run into a jump to cross mat or low apparatus. (2) Show me a tightly curled starting position, next to partner, on your choice of apparatus. Stretch slowly into your fully stretched position, with a contact made. Curl and repeat, keeping time set by new leader. (3) **Climbing frames** Start facing each other on opposite sides of the frame. Can you mirror your travelling actions and several, still, wide body, held positions on one hand and foot only? **Ropes, bench, mats** One partner runs into a strong swing from the mat side, swings over bench, lands on bench, then hands rope to partner. Partner, using a good backward jump up and from the bench, swings to land on mat. Partners have now changed places. Repeat. **Upturned benches, mats** (1) One partner balance walks along the bench, and other partner keeps a gentle hand or hands contact as a support. At two places along the bench, balancer demonstrates a challenging balance, for example on one foot only, and holds it for a few seconds, assisted by his or her partner. Change over. (2) On mats, support your partner in a bent legs headstand. **Trestles** Starting at opposite sides, can you and your partner plan a way to approach each other, meet, pass in an interesting way, then finish in your partner's starting place? **Boxes, mats, bench** Travel and stop, and your following partner will copy and follow.

### FINAL FLOOR ACTIVITY — 2 minutes

The starting leg activity again, because it is so popular and satisfying when you and your partner get it absolutely together.

## NC requirements being emphasised

(a) Working with a partner and developing, refining and evaluating a longer series of actions with and without contact with a partner.

(b) Planning longer sequences and being able to envisage the finished product.

## FLOORWORK

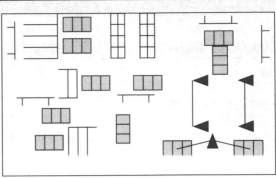

**Legs** If partners are confident that they can 'feel' the rhythm of the jumps, they can be challenged to do four to each side of the room to see if they can finish, facing each other again, 'up and down'.

**Body** (1) Emphasise the whole body involvement in the stretch and the curl. Curl and uncurl, joint by joint, slowly. (2) A sudden change of speed, in arms or hands only, at the very end of stretch or curl, makes an attractive contrast.

**Arms** This is helpful to your partner who doesn't know how he or she looks, inverted in a handstand. Praise one part and mention one part that can be improved.

## APPARATUS WORK

(1) Leader must give following partner good spaces to travel through, keep activities simple, and plan ahead to appropriate actions, apparatus by apparatus. (2) Joint by joint unrolling or curling starts at opposite ends. (From head curling down and in, from feet stretching out and up.) (3) **Climbing frames** Do each method of travelling several times so that your partner can build up to doing it in unison with you, starting and finishing on the floor. **Ropes, benches, mats** Hands together on rope essential for a strong grip as is the upward backward pendulum jump at the start to make a big enough pendulum action to travel the distance easily. **Upturned benches, mats** Try lowering into a horizontal balance standing position with one leg and upper body and arms horizontal. **Trestles** In passing, one can be still, crouched, sitting, hanging under, curled around, for other to go over, around or under. Slowly negotiate and think about body parts concerned. **Boxes, mats, bench** Jumping, rolling, weight on hands and a still balance provide variety and contrasting speeds and effort.

## FINAL FLOOR ACTIVITY

Revise your 'up and down' jumping.

## LESSON PLAN • 30–35 MINUTES

### LESSON THEME

Space awareness and where we are moving, making our movements more interesting, contrasted and individual.

### FLOORWORK                                                      12–15 minutes

**Legs**  Travel on long zig-zags which include movements emphasising going forward, high upwards, and in different directions. Can each part of the zig-zag have a different emphasis? **Body**  (1) Start, crouched close to the floor. Now stretch your whole body to reach as far as possible at a low, medium or high level. Return to your low, curled crouch.  (2) Directions, levels, parts leading the stretch can be varied each time.

**Arms**  (1) Revise handstanding with legs split to make a straight line with one leg ahead and one held back for balance, like a tight rope walker's pole.  (2) Travel on straight legs and arms. Compare the difficulty of travelling with hands and feet wide or together, with body almost horizontal or arched high.

### APPARATUS WORK                                                16–18 minutes

**Climbing frames**  Travel, where you sometimes support yourself close to the apparatus, and sometimes travel well away from it. **Ropes**  (1) Climb vertically up your rope, horizontally across two or more ropes, and vertically or diagonally down. (2) Swing and land three times to show different levels held in the swing and a change of direction somewhere. **Trestles**  Can you travel along, above, across and below the apparatus by bringing hands and feet together and then taking them apart? **Benches, mats**  Zig-zag along the long bench, making hands or feet important. Can you cross the cross bench at a very low or very high level? **Boxes**  Face forward as you vault or cross the cross boxes. On return line of mats, practise sideways or backwards rolls. **Mats**  As a group, with one member setting the rhythm, change from a crouch to a stretch and back to a crouch. Emphasise varied levels with different parts reaching out.

### FINAL FLOOR ACTIVITY                                          2 minutes

On a triangular pathway run forward; jump into a turn; slip sideways; bounce backwards on two feet back to starting place.

## NC requirements being emphasised

(a) Developing sequences showing aesthetic qualities, including variety and contrast.
(b) Suggesting ways of improving quality and degree of difficulty of a performance.

## FLOORWORK

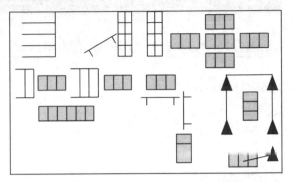

**Legs**  To avoid impeding others, keep each side of the zig zag quite short, 3–4 metres only. 'Long' refers to eventual, total zig zag.
**Body**  (1) A full stretch becomes more difficult as level rises because you run out of supporting surfaces which are plentiful at low levels. (2) A sequence that includes three different supporting parts, in three different directions at three different levels is the challenge. (e.g. Kneeling, stretch upwards; curled on shoulders, stretch both legs sideways; crouched on feet only, stretch to standing on one foot, stretching other leg backwards.)

**Arms**  (1) Foot that pushes from floor stays back and low. Foot that leads movement up on to hands passes the vertical and goes almost horizontal to make a straight line with foot that holds back. (2) Near horizontal body on straight arms and legs, spread wide, is most physically demanding. Travelling on straight arms and legs, close together, is difficult, if you travel, hands only, then feet only.

## APPARATUS WORK

**Climbing frames**  'Close to' sitting, circling, hanging, lowering, pulling, sliding. 'Well away from' crawling action with straight arms and legs; side towards on one foot and hand, alternately. **Ropes**  (1) On the transfer from rope to rope, emphasise the need for a strong hands together grip and a strong, crossed feet grip. (2) Swinging, low level curled; medium level stretched out horizontally; high level legs upwards stretched. **Trestles**  Hands only gripping, pulling, levering, circling. Feet only travel stepping, springing, sliding, circling. **Benches, mats**  Zig zag bounce or spring across bench, without touching it; spring up and across from one or both feet; take weight on hands with bunny jump or cartwheel. **Boxes**  Crouch jump on and spring off; legs between and hand vaults; gate vault, both legs swinging to same side. **Mats**  Group revision of own floorwork practices with emphasis on the group demonstrating a great variety of supporting body parts.

## FINAL FLOOR ACTIVITY

The same start and finish place is easy if sides of triangle are no more than 3 metres long.

## LESSON PLAN • 30–35 MINUTES

### LESSON THEME

Effort and its varied uses to achieve neat, controlled performances. Experiencing different degrees of force, amounts of speed, softness of landings, etc.

### FLOORWORK                                    12–15 minutes

**Legs** (1) Run and jump for height, land and be perfectly still. Repeat a few times, then run and jump for length and stop, still. (2) Experiment to see what is the best speed for accelerating into each kind of jump. (3) How can you help the drive at take-off? **Body** (1) Lie on back, stretched out strongly. (Feel body tension from head and hands down to toes.) Curl up small. Stretch and curl, using slow movements and a variety of levels. (2) Feel the 'firm' stretch each time. **Arms** (1) Try to hold a handstand for three or more seconds using straight arms and spread fingers to control you. (2) Come down softly and under control.

### APPARATUS WORK                              16–18 minutes

**Climbing frames** From a position where part or parts of your body are fixed, travel by pulling, twisting, levering or lowering strongly on to some other part or parts. **Ropes** Revise the leading-up stages to climbing. (a) Swing with hands gripping close, one above the other. (b) Swing with hands together and feet crossed on rope. Rope above one instep, below one sole. (c) Swing with good hand and floor grip and take one hand away to prove a good foot grip. (d) Climb. Hand, hand, hands together, feet up high and grip. **Trestles** Can you transfer from being on the under surfaces to being on the upper surfaces? **Cross bench, bench on bench** At the low, cross bench, leave with hand or hands touching the mat first. Along the high bench, make your hands important. Can you feel the different amounts of energy you are using at the different heights? **Full height box, mats** (1) Approach the high box from a variety of positions. Use your hands strongly as levers to cross, roll along, bring you on to the box. Try to use a good build-up of speed in your run to spring up and across more easily. (2) On landing mats show me a soft controlled landing and a still finish. **Mats** (1) Your stretching and curling sequence, practised on the floor, can be enlarged on the mats where you might do more adventurous movements, such as a stretched handstand into a curled forward roll. (2) Show me your sequence with different levels, using varied supporting parts.

### FINAL FLOOR ACTIVITY                          2 minutes

Crouch, hands and feet on floor. Bounce up on to hands in 'bunny jump'. Roll back to sitting. Rock back up to shoulder balance. Swing back to crouch. Repeat.

## NC requirements being emphasised

**(a)** Understanding factors which influence quality in performances, including body tension. **(b)** Being taught to work hard at activities that develop strength and suppleness.

## FLOORWORK

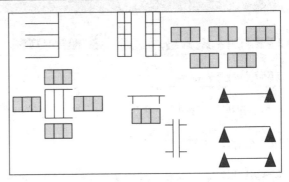

**Legs** (1) Run up for high jump is slower than for long jump, and best from two feet. The quicker long jump take-off is from one foot. (2) High jump medium speed approach is an easy one. The long jump approach builds up quickly for this explosive jump. (3) The high jump is helped by strong swing up of one or both arms. The long jump impetus is from drive by pushing foot at take-off.

**Body** (1) You can stretch on back, side, front, upended on shoulders, kneeling, side falling, arched in a crab, lunging and standing. (2) 'Firm stretch' to an almost larger than life shape, feeling strong and with not a sign of a sagging, lazy body part.

**Arms** (1) Just the right amount of effort is needed to take you up on to, and to hold the hand balance, with arms and hands working hard. (2) The strong energetic move up on to hands is followed by an easy, slow, quiet return to standing.

## APPARATUS WORK

**Climbing frames** Thumbs grip under bar on climber's side, fingers grip over, away from gripper. Split of fingers and thumb is strong unslipping hold. Twist from 'fixed' sitting, standing hanging. **Ropes** Teacher can help by holding feet in the crossed position to give pupil something to push against, in the early stages. **Trestles** While hanging under the pole or plank, co-ordinate push down with one hand on top with opposite leg swing down, or work same hand and leg on to top and round. **Cross bench, bench on bench** From cross bench, cartwheel is difficult. Rolls can be from crouch, kneeling or sitting. Easy bunny jump off answers the challenge satis-

factorily. **Full height box, mats** (1) Simple bunny jumps across; cat spring on, stand and jump off; face vault across; harder roll on to standing, jump off; dive forward roll along full box; gate vault across; hardest through and astride vaults across and along. (2) The softness and the stillness contrast with the previous. **Mats** (1) From the higher handstand, headstand, crab arch stretched, and horizontal balance standing positions, they can more safely try to roll, lower, twist down on to mat into their curls. (2) For example, crouched; stand and stretch to horizontal balance standing; roll forward to sitting; roll back to shoulder balance.

## FINAL FLOOR ACTIVITY

A strong bounce on to hands; gently back to crouch; easy roll back to sitting; strong rock to shoulders; easy long swing back to standing and crouch.

## LESSON PLAN • 30–35 MINUTES

### LESSON THEME

Swinging as an aid and impetus to movement.

### FLOORWORK                                            12–15 minutes

**Legs** (1) On the spot, practise swinging arms up into a stretched jump. Let ankles and knees 'give' for a soft, gentle landing. (2) From a standing position, swing up and twist into a quarter turn. Feel which body parts are creating this twisting jump. (3) Now try a full half turn, starting by twisting your body to the opposite side. The arm, opposite to the side you are going to, can give you an excellent swing into the turn. (4) Swing up into a jump on the spot; run a short distance and swing up into a jump that has a twist in flight or on landing; twist into a quarter or half turn jump to face a new space and start again.
**Body** (1) Start, lying on your back. Twist one part of your body on to another support-

ing part. Twist again. (2) Repeat and emphasise the body part leading into the twist.
**Arms** (1) Swing up on to hands with a long swing of arms, starting above head. In the handstand position, experiment with 'kicking horses' where both legs swing rapidly forward and back, which seems to help balance. (2) With your legs split, one well forward, one held back, on your hands, can you swing the legs to make them change places, so that the leg which swung up first comes down first on to the floor? (3) Can you swing down from your balance with a twist of your lower body to land in a new place?

### APPARATUS WORK                                       16–18 minutes

(1) Travel freely and show me swings up into jumps on the spot and after a short run. Can you swing into jumps that take you across mats and low apparatus? (2) Use apparatus and show me swinging on to and from the different pieces. Swinging on ropes and poles; swing into jumps on to and from benches, planks, mats and boxes; swinging leg or legs up while all body weight is on hands. (3) With your hands as the fixed parts, can you twist on to low apparatus; from most apparatus; to rotate to a lower bar on the climbing

frames; to bring your feet down in a new place generally; and to change direction while swinging on ropes and pole? (4) Now stay at your present apparatus in groups of no more than five or six to practise, improve and remember the following: (a) a still start and finish on the floor away from the apparatus; (b) swings into jumps which can be on the spot, up to, on and down from apparatus, or across lower pieces; (c) fixed hands on apparatus to allow a twisting movement on to, across, from, or within the apparatus itself.

### FINAL FLOOR ACTIVITY                                  2 minutes

Show me a movement using legs where you felt that a swing was a great help to the movement.

## NC requirements being emphasised

(a) Refining and increasing range of gymnastic actions including twisting.

(b) Understanding and assessing how well they and others have achieved what they set out to do, appreciating strengths and limitations.

## FLOORWORK

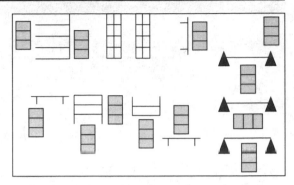

**Legs** (1) As a preparation for the swing up of arms, let body settle with arms going behind back. (2) As a preparation for the twist into turn, let body turn to opposite side first. (3) The bigger the turn, the more important it becomes to drive up strongly with a full ankle extension, to achieve good height. (4) Demonstrate with effective swingers and those with brilliant ankle action, strongly at take-off, softly giving on landing.

**Body** (1) A twist takes place against a fixed point. (2) From lying, twist can be from one arm, lower body fixed; or from one leg, upper body fixed.

**Arms** (1) Years of practising should now be enabling them to achieve the handstand position, which is then hard to hold. The back and forward kicking has been found to be a help. (2) Switching legs while on the hands has also been found to help with retaining the balance a little longer. (3) Pretend you are on a bench and swinging back down to the floor.

## APPARATUS WORK

(1) **Three 'swingings'** Up and forward at start of run; into jump after a short turn, probably on to a mat; and up and across mats and low apparatus. (2) **Swinging on to and from apparatus** Strong legs will be the main swingers on to, or across apparatus. Strong arms will give the lift up and from apparatus. (3) **Hands fixed twisting** Straight arms for a safe, strong action. Grips are very different; hands together on a rope; flat hands on a wide surface; gripping hands on a narrow surface; thumbs under grip on a bar; crossed hands under a pole. (4) **Repeating sequence** *Plan* start and finish places; where to swing into jumps; where to fix hands for the twisting on to, across or from apparatus; and where to do contrasting slower swing or twist.

## FINAL FLOOR ACTIVITY

Good examples of a strong leg or legs swing are the action up on to a handstand, and the action after a run to take you up into a jump. A strong leg swing up into a jump easily takes you into a little turn to face a new direction, helpful if you are approaching a side or end wall.

## LESSON PLAN • 30–35 MINUTES

### LESSON THEME

Partner work which can develop enjoyable and valuable social relationships as well as an awareness and understanding of own and partner's movements. Own movements have to be repeated accurately and partner's movements have to be recognised in detail.

### FLOORWORK                                                    12–15 minutes

**Legs** (1) Follow your leader to all parts of the room, copying the leg movements which change every few seconds. (2) New leader, can you give your following partner some speed, shape or direction changes to observe and copy?
**Body** (1) 'A' holds a clear shape, near to floor level. 'B' clears 'A' and tries to match the shape being held by 'A' (e.g. tuck jump over a curled shape; cartwheel over a star shape).
(2) Change duties.
**Arms** (1) Show your partner a sequence of travelling on one, two or alternate hands. Your partner will watch, then coach you to an even better performance. Repeat, having been helped. (2) Change duties.

### APPARATUS WORK                                              16–18 minutes

**Mats** Show your partner two agilities you enjoy doing, preferably neatly linked and with good start and finish positions. **Climbing frames** One partner travels and stops. The other partner copies and follows. In your sequence as leader, can you include: (**a**) varied, whole body movements; (**b**) varied pathways, e.g. zig-zag; vertical; diagonal or horizontal? **Ropes, bench, mats** Partners work side by side to develop a matching sequence with a clear body shape throughout.
**Trestles** Start at opposite ends of the apparatus. Approach, meet, pass, and finish in partner's starting place. Can you include a direction change somewhere? **Cross bench, mats** Running, jumping and landing from opposite sides. Build up to a matching sequence in unison, trying to show vigorous action one way and a more gentle action the other way. **Boxes, mats, return bench** Follow your leader, trying to keep some contact between you at several points. (e.g. Jump down together, hand held; assisted jumps, side to side, over bench.)

### FINAL FLOOR ACTIVITY                                            2 minutes

Following one just behind and to one side of other, make a matching sequence to include travelling, flight, balance and an inversion.

## NC requirements being emphasised

Working with a partner and being given guidance and opportunity to develop, refine and evaluate a series of actions with and without contact with a partner.

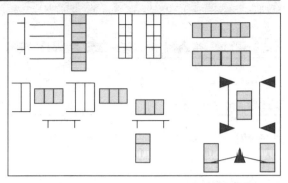

## FLOORWORK

**Legs** (1) A simple 'follow the leader' with leader and follower thinking 'What actions and what uses of body parts?' (2) New leader can retain the series of actions already worked on, but embellish them as he or she thinks 'What body shapes, or changes of speed or direction are appropriate additions?'

**Body** (1) Low level partner 'A' can give partner some easy starting shapes to encourage quick action (e.g. lying, long and straight, wide or curled for partner 'B' to jump over in the same shape). (2) With the lesson's progress, week by week, the still partner can hold shapes that encourage work on hands by the moving partner.

**Arms** (1) Partner will look for good, still start and finish positions; well controlled actions, done slowly; and good body shapes with straight arms and feet together, for example, in a handstand. (2) Observing partner should also comment on a feature that is thought to be pleasing, as an encouragement.

## APPARATUS WORK

**Mats** 'Agilities' means the emphasis is on hand supported. When the emphasis is on feet, it is called 'vaulting.' **Climbing frames** Each should be aware of, and able to list the 'What?' – the varied, large body movements used – and the 'Where?' – the pathways and the directions being followed. **Ropes, bench, mats** For example, side by side, still starting position on bench; swing forward, back and forward to land on mat, still holding rope in one hand; balance on one leg, upper body angled to horizontal; drop rope and forward roll across mat. **Trestles** At moment of passing each other, it is a good idea for one to be stationary, curled on or under, across or around, or standing for partner to negotiate, carefully past. **Cross bench, mats** A starting signal can be a lifting on one partner's heels. Same foot starts the run in and strikes the bench. Same shape in flight and same landing action. The ultimate is a strike on bench at exactly the same time. **Boxes, mats, return bench** Leader should travel a little distance, then stop, while follower stands watching the actions. Following partner catches up, then remains still, watching the next part.

## FINAL FLOOR ACTIVITY

For example, heels raising starting signal; short travel of five strides; identical flight with swing up of one arm; land one foot after the other, slowly; balance on one foot; lower to sitting to shoulder balance; swing up to standing. Repeat.

## LESSON PLAN • 30–35 MINUTES

### LESSON THEME

Sequences and performances that show the development in skilfulness, knowledge and understanding that have taken place during the four year course in Gymnastic Activities.

### FLOORWORK                                                                    12–15 minutes

**Legs** (1) In your sequence of varied ways to travel on your feet, can you plan to include: (**a**) a still, poised start and finish; (**b**) a jump at beginning or end; (**c**) a change of direction somewhere?
**Body** In your sequence of body movements, each taken to its limits (e.g. tightest bend; fullest stretch; widest star), can you include: (**a**) moment of stillness with non supporting parts stretched; (**b**) changes of levels?
**Arms** In your sequence on hands, can you include: (**a**) different ways to move on to hands; (**b**) different ways of moving while on hands; (**c**) clear and varied body shapes; (**d**) a stretched, still start and finish?

### APPARATUS WORK                                                              16–18 minutes

**Climbing frames** (1) Can you balance, travel, balance showing a variety of supporting body parts in the balances with non-supporting parts stretched? (2) Can you include body vertical, horizontal, upended or with front, back or side towards the floor? **Ropes** Can you: (**a**) climb your rope three times; (**b**) show me a sequence of swings to include varied landing actions, shapes and a change of direction? **Trestles** Can you include: (**a**) movements above and below the apparatus; (**b**) a variety of supporting parts; (**c**) being upended somewhere? **Upturned benches, bench on trestle, trestle, mats** In your sequence of balances, can you include: (**a**) different levels; (**b**) different supporting parts; (**c**) neat linking movements between one balance and the next on a new piece of apparatus? **Low, long box, high cross box, mats** In your sequence along long box and mat, and back over cross box and mat, can you include: (**a**) gymnastic links between the end of one line and the start of the next (cartwheel, roll, jump, etc.); (**b**) a direction change; (**c**) a vigorous movement at speed? **Mats** Show me a favourite sequence of at least three agilities, all neatly linked.

### FINAL FLOOR ACTIVITY                                                         2 minutes

In this, your very last sequence, please show me: (**a**) favourite ways to travel on feet; (**b**) a body movement you enjoy performing; (**c**) your best activity on one, two or alternate hands.

## NC requirements being emphasised

(a) Planning longer sequences and able to envisage the finished product.

(b) Trying hard to consolidate their performances.

## TEACHING POINTS

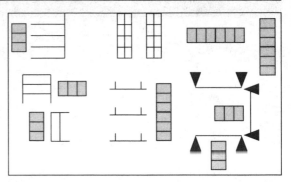

In NC terms, the pupils work should have continually involved them in *planning*, which prepares the way for their thoughtful, focused *participation*. Teacher comment, and class comment following demonstrations, then inspire the *reflection and evaluation* which assist the performers and the observers to plan and adapt, as necessary, to bring about improvement in the next set of performances, and so the process continues.

Gymnastic Activities is a visual, doing subject. We remember what we see and the pupils should have seen hundreds of demonstrations of good movement. We learn by doing and the pupils will have spent about 80 hours doing Gymnastic Activities in their primary school. In this, the last lesson in their primary (middle) school, the class are recalling and presenting favourite ways of travelling, moving, balancing, and jumping on floor and on to and from apparatus. It is hoped that they are also presenting perspiring, smiling faces.

Their achievement in terms of skilfulness is expressed in well controlled, poised and versatile movement. Well planned performances use the space well and include those elements of 'movement' which enhance the work and make it more interesting, exciting and pleasing. Such elements include contrast, variety, repetition, good body tension and clear body shapes.

Their achievement in terms of knowledge and understanding is expressed in their extensive repertoire, the way that actions are linked together, and their effective and appropriate use of the 'movement' enhancing features listed above.

It is hoped that they have also developed a healthy attitude to participation in regular and vigorous physical activity which is expressed in consistently wholehearted and enthusiastic involvement, exuding a sense of self-assured enjoyment and satisfaction.

# INDEX